"*The Knock* ⌐.   ; and intriguing read. You will not be disappointed."

—*Armenian Weekly*

"In *The Knock at the Door*, Ester's daughter has captured the haunting details of her mother's compelling story. The author invites us into her family circle, offering a fascinating glimpse of the Armenian culture and its painful history."

—Governor Hugh L. Carey

"A riveting, draining and reflective account of how people prevail over awful fortunes."

—*Kirkus*

". . . A moving yet deeply disturbing account. Ahnert has provided an invaluable service by putting human faces on the victims."

—*Booklist*

"This memoir puts the tragic Armenian experience in personal terms and reminds us Americans of one early genocide as we try to respond to repeated global disasters. Recommended for its deft balance between personal story and historic tragedy."

—*Library Journal*

"Margaret Ahnert has written an incredibly moving recollection of her mother's ordeal as a young girl during the Armenian Genocide in Turkey. Of all the books and articles I have read on this terrible era, her account rings true, perhaps because it issues from one source—the eyewitness memories of her ninety-eight-year-old mother. Read this book. You will cry, you will laugh. And you will know the truth."

—Bill Henderson, Pushcart Press

"In *The Knock at the Door*, Margaret Ahnert has skillfully recreated her mother's traumatic battle to survive the Armenian Genocide in Turkey during World War I. The story, pieced together with notes from conversations and tape recordings of her mother, is observed with great sensitivity through her mother's eyes in a way that is genuine and overwhelming in its controlled and contained narrative."

—Lee Gutkind, Professor of English at the University of Pittsburgh, author of *Almost Human: Making Robots Think*

"Margaret Ahnert's book, *The Knock at the Door*, made me laugh, cry, and also opened my heart and soul to what cruelty the Armenian Genocide in Turkey brought to millions of harmless families. Read this book and get to know Ester, Margaret's mother, and pray that a little of her wisdom and courage rubs off on you after you've read it. It's a MUST READ!"

—Mary Occhino, author of *Beyond These Four Walls*, and *Sign of the Dove*

THE KNOCK AT THE DOOR

THE KNOCK AT THE DOOR

A Mother's Story of Surviving the Armenian Genocide

Margaret Ajemian Ahnert

BEAUFORT BOOKS
NEW YORK

FIRST EDITION 2007
FIRST PAPERBACK EDITION 2012

Paperback ISBN: 978-0-8253-0683-9

Library of Congress Cataloging-in-Publication Data

Ahnert, Margaret Ajemian.
  The knock at the door : a journey through the darkness of the Armenian genocide / Margaret Ajemian Ahnert.
    p. cm.
  ISBN 978-0-8253-0512-2 (alk. paper)
  1. Armenian massacres, 1915-1923 — Personal narratives. 2. Ajemian, Ester Minerajian, b. 1900. 3. Ahnert, Margaret Ajemian. 4. Armenian-Americans--Biography. I. Title.

  DS195.5.A385 2007
  956.6'20154--dc22
  [B]

                              2006101535

DISCLAIMER

Although there is a great deal of information available to the general public concerning the Armenian genocide, the stories told herein are based solely on the memories of my mother, who lived through it. As a result of the horrific events that took place and the lack of documentary evidence, a great deal of my mother's stories cannot be specifically verified. In addition, some names and characteristics of individuals have been changed or altered. Over the years, I took notes and made recordings of her stories. Even through she repeated these stories many times, she never altered the details. The stories in this book are the stories she told me in her limited English. The words and the voice in the stories are mine.

Map produced by the Armenian National Institute (ANI) (Washington, D.C.) and the Nubarian Library (Paris). © ANI, English Edition Copyright 1998.

Published in the United States by Beaufort Books, New York
www.beaufortbooks.com
Distributed by Midpoint Trade Books, New York
www.midpointtradebooks.com

Jacket design by Amy C. King
Jacket photograph by Superstock
Author photograph by Claus Mroczysk

10 9 8 7 6 5 4 3 2 1

PRINTED IN THE UNITED STATES OF AMERICA

This book is dedicated to my mother, Ester,
the most courageous person I've ever known,
whose recollections and vivid memory
helped me write this book.
Her voice is with me still.

For God shall bring every work into judgment,
with every secret thing,
whether it be good,
or whether it be evil.

— *Ecclesiastes 12:14*

CONTENTS

PROLOGUE

My mother wanted me to marry an Armenian, and I did. His name was Steve, a kind, gentle young man. Although I did grow to love him, the choice was not mine. In those days — the 1950s — I dared not disappoint my mother, who, in the end, wanted only one thing from me — that I marry an Armenian and carry on our bloodline. People say blood is thicker than water, and I know this to be literally true. Water is just plain old hydrogen and oxygen, but blood — it's packed with platelets, proteins, and DNA.

I'm in my fifties now, remarried — with two beautiful children and two grandchildren who know little of the history and the genocide their great-grandmother survived.

Their great grandmother, my mother, Ester, was only 15 when the Armenian Genocide began. More than one million Armenians were killed by the end of it.

Mother is dying now. So am I, I suppose. As I age, I get all the expected ailments. The other day, the doctor diagnosed me with a mostly benign condition of — what else — the blood. My blood has too many platelets in it, raising my stroke risk. Now I must take two tiny pink aspirin every day. I don't mind. I like to think I have too much blood, and that I am brimming with my mother, and me, and all we carry, together.

Ester, my father Albert, Steve, and George, my high school sweetheart — the one I didn't marry — and all the people I know through my mother's stories — they all come crowding back in my thoughts when I bike or walk in an area called "The Pines." A dirt road surrounded by tall pine trees, The Pines is a special place on the tiny island of Bimini off the Florida coast, where my husband Bob and I like to fish.

Some scholars say the lost continent of Atlantis lies beneath the island and that Bimini may be one of its mountain peaks. Whatever it is, when I'm near The Pines, I feel an energy, a sense of presence, churchlike, holy. I cannot explain.

Sometimes, when I'm there, I talk out loud to my father, who died when I was thirteen. I remind him of the question I asked him as a child. Why don't I have any aunts or uncles or cousins like the other kids in school? Why, one of my friends even had a cousin's club with three hundred members. I didn't have a single relative on either my father's or my mother's side. As a child, Papa ignored my question with the simple word, *mortseer!* But how could I forget what I never knew? I tell my father, "Now, I know."

It wasn't until I was seventeen and first read Franz Werfel's *The Forty Days of Musa Dagh,* an account of one Armenian

village's stand against the Turkish army, that I started to understand. I was working as a secretary at a Wall Street brokerage
firm. At noon each day I'd stroll the short distance up Wall Street
to Broadway and enter the Trinity Church graveyard. I carried
my lunch and Werfel's book in a brown paper bag. I ate alone.

Sitting on a stone grave marker in the shape of a colonial
chair, I ate my lunch and immersed myself in my heritage. I de-
voured Werfel's book while the passing parade of bankers and
moneymaking wizards hurried to their next deal. I sat quietly
amongst the dead, unnoticed.

As I read, the characters came alive for me. The Bagradians, central figures in Werfel's novel, were uprooted and perse-
cuted by the Turks, as Mother and her family had been. It was
a family by the name of Bagradian who took in Mother. I
wondered, could they be related?

The characters — in fact, the entire novel — disturbed
the Turkish government so much that in 1935, when Metro-
Goldwyn-Mayer announced it was making a film of the novel,
the Turkish ambassador asked the U.S. secretary of state to
block the release of the film. It was never produced.

Reading this book changed my life. I began to ask about
the "dark time," a time my mother had lived through and tried
to forget.

I searched through old history books and learned that the
Armenians and the Turks had lived contiguously in relative
peace since the tenth century. What happened to change this? I
learned that, in the 1890s, Sultan Abdul Hamid began to en-
courage wholesale attacks on Armenian communities. He
viewed the Armenians as a group with dangerous nationalistic
goals. Their religion and their prosperity made them natural
objects of xenophobia. The Christian Armenians were forbidden to bear arms.

Henry Morgenthau, the residing United States ambassador to Turkey, in his memoir, *Ambassador Morgenthau's Story*, described the Turkish nation as "the sick man of Europe." In 1908, a trio calling themselves the Union and Progress Committee, also known as the Young Turks, took power.

Morgenthau said this ruling triumvirate — Enver Pasha, Talaat Bey, and Djemal Pasha — was more ruthless than even the regime of Abdul Hamid. These three set the genocide of the Armenians in motion.

The Ambassador described the operation as efficient and brutal. Before 1915, there had been about two and a half million Armenians living in Turkey. After the murders and the tortures of the death march, only one-third remained. A handful had escaped over the frontiers into Russia and the Arab territories. The Young Turks' campaign exterminated nearly one third of all the Armenians in the world.

Ambassador Morgenthau writes: "I find in my diary on August 3rd that, 'Talaat is the one who desires to crush the poor Armenians.' He told me that the Committee of Union and Progress had fully considered the matter in all its details and that the policy which was being pursued was that which they had officially adopted. 'Why are you so interested in the Armenians, anyway?' Talaat said on another occasion, 'You are a Jew; these people are Christians. The Mohammedans and the Jews always get on harmoniously. We are treating the Jews here all right. What have you to complain of?'

"'You don't seem to realize,' I replied, 'that I am not here as a Jew but as the American Ambassador.'

"'We treat the Americans all right, too,' said Talaat. 'I don't see why you should complain.'"

When his efforts to intervene failed, Morgenthau attempted to put pressure on the Turks through the German Ambassador, who wrote back: "I have lived in Turkey the larger part of my life, and I know the Armenians. I also know that both Armenians and Turks cannot live together in this country. One of these races has got to go. And I don't blame the Turks for what they are doing to the Armenians. I think that they are entirely justified. The weaker nation must succumb."

I needed more information. I looked up Armenian history in the library. Everything I read about Armenia told me that the ancient Armenians had lived continuously in large parts of what is now Turkey for over two thousand years. I was surprised to learn that the Armenians were the first nation to accept Christianity.

St. Gregory the Illuminator converted King Tirades in 301 A.D. and the Romans followed several years later. I asked my friend, a Roman Catholic priest, if he knew this fact. "I always thought the Romans were the first Christians," I said to him.

"Many people believe that Rome was the first to espouse Christianity: the truth is the Armenians were the first as a nation," my friend said.

A patriotic chord stirred in my psyche.

As I read, I learned that during the atrocities in 1915, Armenians were rounded up, tortured, and murdered. On April 24, 1915, the deportations of the Armenian intellectuals and leaders in Constantinople began. Later in May and June, an order went out that all Armenians aged five and up who were Ottoman subjects were to be taken out of the towns and slaughtered. Mother and her family were uprooted in June. There was even an edict that Armenians serving in the Turkish army were to be segregated and shot.

I was stunned! Mother had told me about her brother, Haroutoun, who was a soldier in the Turkish Army. Was he marched out of town and killed like the rest? I needed to know more.

What was the rest of the world doing at this time? Didn't they know? Weren't they told? Was anyone reporting what they saw?

A headline in *The New York Times* on August 18, 1915, said, ARMENIANS ARE SENT TO PERISH IN DESERT, and then on August 27, TURKS DEPOPULATE TOWNS OF ARMENIA. On September 17, a headline read, MISSION BOARD TOLD OF TURKISH HORRORS; CORRESPONDENTS CONFIRM THE REPORTS OF THE WIPING OUT OF ARMENIANS.

Was this genocide? It wouldn't have been called that in 1915, as the word had not yet entered the lexicon. That wouldn't happen until after Hitler's planned extermination of the Jews.

What exactly does the word mean, anyway, I wondered. I pulled the dictionary from the shelf. Genocide: "The deliberate and systematic extermination of a nation, racial, political, or cultural group." If this was not genocide in 1915, what was it? Deliberate and systematic were the key words for me.

To this day, scholars can't agree on what the motives of the Turkish government were: perhaps Turkey was never able to assimilate the different nationalities that were a part of its empire. Perhaps the Turks were punishing the Armenians for being Christians. Or perhaps genocides occur for no real reason, a dent in the biology of our brains, some evolutionary adaptive strategy run amok. Of one thing I am sure. As people, we are full of snags and rust.

I leaned forward when I read in Louis Lochner's book, *What About Germany,* "In 1939, when Adolf Hitler was questioned about his plan to kill all men, women, and children of

Poland, he answered, 'Who, after all, speaks today of the anni-hilation of the Armenians?'" Today, this telling quote is dis-played prominently in the United States Holocaust Memorial Museum in Washington, D.C.

The Talmud says "he who saves one life saves the world in time." Had the world stopped the insanity in 1915, would there have been a Holocaust in 1942? The answer is clear — at least to me.

Jews and Armenians suffered the same plight. Eventually, Germany acknowledged its crimes. Yet even today, Turkey is unrepentant, and these crimes remain unpunished.

My mother survived, and fled to America in her adolescent years. Now in her nineties, she lives in an Armenian home for old people in New York. What she has are her memories, which are many, and her regrets, which are few.

I write, not for revenge, but for the record: of my mother, of me.

The other day, when I was visiting her, she leaned her head back on the chair rest, closed her eyes, and said, "I remember the day you married Steve. We were in Philadelphia. You were such a beautiful bride but you didn't smile. You cried that day, and I put the reason right out of my head."

"Mother, that was years ago," I said.

"I know, but my heart is heavy. I want you to know I'm sorry. I wanted one of my children to carry on the Armenian tradition. But I was wrong. It was wrong. It was selfish of me. You know, I did the best I could. I'm sorry if I made mistakes. I want you to know this."

"It's all right, Mother, I understand. I had a good life with Steve, two wonderful children and two grandchildren. I know now that it was the right thing to do."

"You're a good girl. You always did what I asked. God will reward you someday."

"He already has, Mother," I said. I thought of my children, the skeins of strength that ran through me, the skeins of strength that she gave me, her world, so storied and full.

And so this book was born. Each visit to New York, Mother recounted her childhood stories as vividly as she had when I was a child. These pages document her life as she told it to me. She was the narrator. I was her scribe.

Every scribe leaves a trace of himself in the work.

This is the story of us, told together.

THE KNOCK AT THE DOOR

The 1915 Armenian Genocide in the Turkish Empire

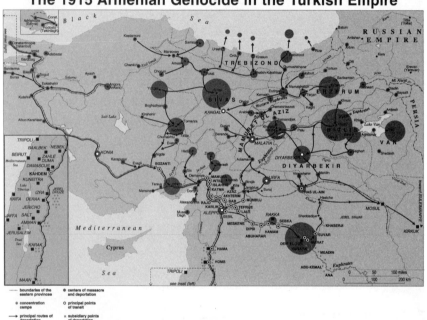

boundaries of the eastern provinces

concentration camps

principal routes of deportation

rail lines

centers of massacre and deportation

principal points of transit

subsidiary points of deportation

principal destination points of deportation

ONE

A PAPER CROWN

MARGARET — MARCH 1998

Icy rain splashed against the small square window of the Boeing jet as it came to a sliding stop at La Guardia Airport. I remember it was March and it was cold. March 12, 1998, my mother's ninety-eighth birthday. In my lap I held two dozen red roses, Mother's favorite flowers. Suffering from the remnants of the flu, my head was pounding, my nose running.

Outside, the freezing air stung my face. Ice beaded on my moist lashes. I lived in Florida, where it was always warm, the beach white as a baby's bedsheet.

"Taxi, lady? Any luggage?"

"No, no luggage," I said, as I snuggled in the back seat, hoping the heat was on. It wasn't.

1

"Where to?"

"The Armenian Home." I handed him the address.

"Yeah, I know where this is. I've been driving a cab in this neighborhood for forty years. You picked the right cab. A lot of these new guys can't speak English and don't know the neighborhood."

He was slender, gray, and chewed gum with an irritating clicking sound. He smelled like a Nathan's hot dog and Aqua Velva cologne. He had a pleasant smile.

Seymour Berman was the name on his ID. Checking the names of taxi drivers was a habit I had acquired when I lived in New York. It was both a safety factor and a human-interest device. Sometimes if a name sounded Armenian, I would ask the driver if he were of Armenian descent. If so, we'd talk about Armenian food, music, and what part of the old country his family came from.

Once, a driver with an Armenian sounding name said he was Turkish.

"Are you Armenian?" he asked.

I hid my trembling hands deep in my pockets. Beads of sweat broke out on my forehead and inched down my nose. I was afraid to tell him I was Armenian.

"No, no I'm not, but I have an Armenian friend and she told me that 'ian' at the end of a name means the name could possibly be Armenian."

Why did I deny my heritage? Why was I afraid of this Turkish cab driver?

I shrugged off this memory as Mr. Berman wove his way through the back streets, narrowly missing pedestrians, trucks, and pushcarts filled with fresh produce. Shoppers carried large bags filled with loaves and fruits: tomatoes as red as Christmas ornaments, cantaloupes in their ridged sealed skins. Mother carried her groceries the same way many years ago.

I remember a street like this. I lived with my parents, Ester and Albert Ajemian, in The Bronx. Even though I had two sisters, Rose and Alice, I felt like an only child, as they were much older than me and we had little in common.

It was the 1940s, when shopping for food was a daily chore. Meat and chickens were fresh, not frozen. Piles of produce were loaded on stands to be closely inspected by housewives determined to handpick the best bright green spinach, taut yellow squash, and green beans.

Dozens of chickens raced around in a wire pen without a notion of their scheduled execution. Once Mother asked me to choose a chicken. A burly man with black hair sticking out in so many angles he looked like a porcupine leaned over his blood-splattered apron and picked up the chicken I had chosen. Holding my chicken by the neck with one hand, he slashed off its head. It rolled to one side of the sawdust-covered floor. Blood gushed from the chicken. I did not eat dinner that night. I never picked another chicken.

The taxi pulled into the circular drive of what had once been a stately mansion. Now, tall apartment buildings surrounded the old house. From their windows hung lines of colorful wash flowing in the blustery wind like flags. The house must have been grand in its day, but today the stained, worn mortar between the old brick was barely visible under the overgrown ivy draping the cracks. The paint on the windows was a little chipped but the surrounding shrubbery showed the gentle care of a knowledgeable caretaker. A sign in the front announced it as an old age home. The paneled front door was freshly painted. Pale colonial blue columns flanked the clean white door.

"*Your mother is in the solarium,*" *the receptionist said.* "*We didn't tell her you were coming,*"

"*Why not?*"

"*Sometimes people say they are coming and don't. I've seen residents cry when their family doesn't show up.*"

She pointed me toward the solarium and walked away, the scent of White Shoulders trailing behind her. I walked through the first room beyond the reception area and noticed several elderly women and one man. They sat in wooden armchairs staring ahead but seemed not to be waiting for anything. I needed air. I stepped back outside.

The leafless oak trees in the garden were covered with a thin veil of white frost. Long branches intertwined and mingled. They looked like a mass of twisted bony arms and legs. These mangled trees reminded me of the mounds of bodies I saw in photographs of the Armenian Genocide of 1915.

A heavy gray atmosphere hung over the yard. I took a deep breath. The air smelled sweet and fresh as it sometimes does before a snowfall. I wondered how soon would it start? How many inches would fall? Did it snow in Amasia, the town in Turkey where Mother was born? I needed to get hold of myself.

I stepped back inside. I rounded the entry hall to the solarium and stood in the center of the room, letting the hazy glow of the afternoon sun wash over my body. Worn green leather armchairs lined the walls. Fresh varnish added a soft luster to the well-worn asphalt tile floors. Banquet-style tables, rows of wooden chairs clustered in groups of four and six, were scattered throughout the spacious room.

Just inside the solarium to the right of the doorway stood an elaborate altar, one that any church would be proud to own. A stiffly starched crocheted scarf was draped neatly across its flat surface. Evenly spaced were two candelabras, an incense holder, leather-bound Bible with a gold-embossed cross on the cover, and a Communion cup covered with a white linen napkin. Every Sunday, Mass was held in this room for the residents.

I saw Mother. She was sitting with a thin, gray-haired lady off to one side of the large room away from the others. Mother's hair was very short and straight. Her soft curly bob was gone. This was not the way she liked to wear it. I walked towards her and started to say, who cut your hair? Why did you let them cut it so short?

Instead, I said nothing.

"Margaret, is that you? Yes, yes, it is! Look, everyone, my daughter Margaret is here," she said in Armenian, clapping her hands like a child. "She's come all the way from Florida to see me."

Then, as if an afterthought she turned to me and said, "Or did you drive in from your house in Pennsylvania? My daughter has two houses," Mother boasted to the women within earshot. "I'm so happy to see you."

Mother was speaking Armenian to everyone. Most of her life she spoke English, but here in this Armenian home for the aged she had reverted to the language of her birth. Mother, the chameleon. On a moment's notice she could switch her languages to fit her surroundings.

That's the key, I thought. That's how she survived. She knew how to adapt. Always living her life in the present moment, she accepted situations beyond her control and reacted accordingly. This was her gift. She told me many times, "It's not what happens to you in life that's important, it's how you react to it. You must take the good with the bad and never look back."

Mother seemed so small, so fragile. Though her eyes sparkled with enthusiasm, her skin was old and thin. It was as if her bones were covered with parchment paper. She gulped air into her frail chest. I cradled her bony, wax-like hand in mine. Her skin was more wrinkled than I had remembered it. I clasped my fingers around hers.

"Ouch. That hurts!" she said. I let go. She reached for my hand again. She needed to touch me. I put the roses down and gently covered her hands with both of mine.

Mother picked up the flowers from her lap, raised them to her nose, and sniffed.

"Umm," she said. "They smell like the roses of Amasia. They, too, were red."

"Come sit by my knee like you used to when you were a little girl," Mother said.

I had forgotten how it felt to be a little girl. Some mornings, my body creaking with early signs of arthritis, I doubted I'd ever been one. Mother, who survived genocide, smiled at me with childlike joy. There were tears in my eyes. My mother was brave. Even though she was living with strangers, out of her own home, she still appeared happy.

Mother patted my shoulder, "Now, now, why are you crying? This is a happy day. Today is my birthday."

An aide brought in a large gold paper crown with colored stones glued on it and placed it on Mother's head. She was the birthday guest of honor. Armenian music was playing on a black boom box, the kind that kids use.

"Let's dance, Ester," said a tall, buxom nurse, catching my hand and Mother's. Suddenly, in the middle of the great solarium, we were dancing and others joined us. I watched as the skeletal forms moved slowly around the room, waving their

arms to the beat of the music. A woman in a wheelchair was weaving her upper body in perfect sync with the rhythm.

I stopped dancing and watched Mother. Using her walker for balance she, too, was dancing. Dancing! It had only been weeks since she had broken her hip, and we brought her here. What was the secret of her resilience? Did constant pain and hardship make one stronger? How curious it all seemed.

Yet, as I watched the dancing, weaving and clapping, I realized that here in this old age home, mother had come full circle. Back to her roots, back among people whose lives had also been interrupted in 1915, when the Turkish government set about to rid Turkey of all Armenians. Was the safety that she felt in this home so comforting that she spoke her birth language without fear? Did she feel more secure here than at any other time in her life? The residents seemed to have a common bond here, in the safety of their surroundings. They talked and listened to each other. Each had a story to tell.

"You know, Margaret," Mother said, "everyone here believes that what happened to them was the worst of the massacre stories. If you listen long enough you will see that each person's hell was not very different than his neighbors'. We all suffered," she said. "It was all such a long time ago. We talk, we remember, we eat."

"It's time for more singing, hand-clapping, and picture-taking," I hear an aide say. Candles are lit. We sing "Happy Birthday" in Armenian. I see myself in Mother's place in another time. I am wearing a jeweled, gold paper crown and I am alone. I can feel the weight of the crown on my head.

When I was a child, Mother told me stories that had a profound impact on my life. She described the death camps, the starvation, and the torture she had witnessed. Always, the details of the stories were the same. I grew up with a deep sense of fear of all Turks.

I remember one cold day in December, I returned home from elementary school to find my mother crying and swaying back and forth in the living room. A button was missing from her faded gray wool sweater. A sad Armenian song played on the record player. She didn't see or notice me at first, but when she did, she turned her head in my direction, put two fingers to her lips, and whispered, "Shhhhhhh." Then she turned her head away, stared blankly ahead and continued her chanting, "There is no one left. They are all dead."

My father arrived home early that day and caught this scene: Mother wailing and me cowering in a corner watching her.

"What's the matter with you?" he said. "It's all over; you're safe here in America. Stop scaring the child. She must not know about 'the trouble.' She must grow up as an American. Stop this crying right now. Mortseer!" he said again and again. Mortseer.

Mother wiped her eyes with the back of her hand, turned off the record player, and through clenched teeth she hissed, "I cannot forget! I will not forget! They killed them all."

Not all of the stories mother told me as a child were about the "dark time." She also shared wonderful, joyous tales about school, summer trips to the family aikee, where they had a cottage among the orchards. She described holidays, weddings, and visits to the local bathhouse. Her life was so different from mine.

Now Mother lived in room 202 on the second floor of the old age home. Perched in the corner of a red leather chair near the door, she sat quietly with her hands folded in her lap.

I sat on her bed, leaned over to her, and murmured, "Why

didn't you stay in Amasia and marry a Turk if that could have saved you from the death march? If I had been there I would have married a Turk, waited for the right moment, perhaps even killed the beast in his sleep, and then escaped to join the revolutionaries in Russia."

"Some of my schoolmates did just that," Mother said. "They married local Turks and became Turkish. No, I could not do what they did. The price was too high. They were forbidden to speak the Armenian language, and worst of all, they were forbidden to pray to their Christian God. No, I couldn't do that. I could not deny my God. I'm not sorry I left."

But then, as if in an afterthought, she said, "Maybe you're right. But, if I had not left, I would not be here today. You wouldn't be here."

"Well," I answered haughtily. "I might have been a Turkish princess laden with riches."

"You are a princess," Mother replied. "Okay, Princess, help me get into bed. I'm tired."

I fumbled through my purse. I had a surprise for Mother. In an out-of-print book given to me by a friend, I'd found a picture of mother's town of Amasia. In the glow of setting sunlight, I sat mother up in her bed and showed her the picture.

"Can you recognize your house in this photo?"

"Oh, my God! Where did you get this picture?"

Her pupils were clouded with cataracts. She held the photo close to her face.

"I lived on the other side of this river in the Savaieet sector. You can't see my house in this picture, but I know just where it is," she said. "What a wonderful happy memory you have given me. Margaret, you are such a good girl." She rubbed my cheek with her bony fingers.

"When you were a young child you always asked me

about my life in the old country. Now that I see you with children of your own, I realize how important memories of the past are. When I die, the truth will die with me. You must know and your children must know what I lived through."

I leaned closer, "Mother, do you hate the Turks today for what they did to you and your family?"

Mother simply and quickly answered, "No, I don't."

"Why not? They took your house, your possessions, your land and killed your entire family. How could you not hate them?"

"I don't know why," she said. "The Turks always hated us. They hated us because we were Christians. They called us giavours, infidels. I know it sounds strange but I feel no hatred for the Turks. God will judge them, not me. Margaret, do not fill your life with hate. It will only hurt you. Hatred is like acid, it burns through the container. You must let go of bad memories."

I wiped mother's sweaty brow. Her face twitched.

"Do whatever you want to do in life now. Don't wait. There is nothing later. I know that."

"How do you know there is nothing later? Maybe there is an afterlife somewhere."

"Maybe," she said, "but I'll be too old to enjoy it."

"Well, maybe you'll be young again in the next life."

Mother smiled, then said, "I'll let you know."

I kissed her cheek. It was soft and smelled of the baby lotion I had rubbed on her face and arms. I plucked four long black hairs from her face with my tweezers.

"Here, don't miss this one," she said, pointing to one under her chin.

I clipped, filed, and polished her fingernails as she watched me intently.

"Be careful," she said. "Don't drop any pieces on the floor. If someone steps on them, I'll have bad luck."

At ninety-eight, Mother's luck had served her well. I wasn't going to take any chances. I carefully collected the little moon-shaped bits, wrapped them tightly in a tissue, and safely placed them in the wastebasket.

"This is how I took care of you when you were a baby," she said. "It's nice to have you taking care of me now. I love the feel of your hands rubbing my body. I used to rub you down with baby oil and dangle you upside down from your ankles. Do you think you can flip me in the air by my ankles?"

"No, Mother, I'm sure I cannot flip you around by your ankles. Why did you do that to me?"

"Well, in the old country, the old women said if you flipped a child upside down by his ankles he would grow up to be very smart. I guess it worked. You're pretty smart."

I smiled.

"I hope your children take care of you like you are taking care of me," Mother whispered.

I blew my nose. My head was burning. Mother slowly blinked her eyes. This visit was tiring her.

"Why didn't God step in and save the Armenians?" I suddenly said out loud.

Mother shrugged her shoulders. "Who knows why? Only God knows. When I see him, I'll ask him."

"Did you ever think about killing yourself?"

"Of course."

"Why didn't you do it?"

"I don't know why. I surely wanted to die. I guess deep down we all want to live, no matter how bad life is. Life is what we make of what God gives us."

She continued, "Margaret, you must never give up hope.

11

No matter what happens to you, you must remember to have faith and hope. Hope kept me alive."

I looked at my watch. It was 4:40 P.M. I had to rush if I was going to catch the 6 o'clock flight back to Florida. I kissed mother goodbye. She reached for my face and pulled me close. I worried that it might be the last time I'd see her alive.

"I love you," she said. "I'll always love you, promise me you will remember this."

"I promise."

Once on the plane, I took a deep breath, the kind Mother taught me how to take. I shut my eyes and tried to remember the good times in Mother's life.

TWO

EARLY MEMORIES

ESTER — 1905–1912

Quietly nestled in one of the interior provinces of Turkey lies my beautiful town of Amasia. On one of the side streets in the Savaieet Armenian sector was my house. My story begins back in 1905, when I was five. I don't remember much about my family. I was told I was born Ester Minerajian on March 12, 1900, and that my mother died birthing me, her seventh child.

Shortly after she died, my father, who was very sick, gave my six brothers and sisters and me to his brother for care. This brother promised to raise us as a family, so my father gave him his house, all his personal wealth, and my mother's jewels. After my father died, my uncle went back on his word and gave us all up for adoption. I never saw my brothers and sisters again, except for one, my oldest brother Haroutoun.

When I was five I was adopted by Hajji Hagop Ahronian and his wife, Pepron. This was one of the leading families in Amasia. My new father had the title of "Hajji." This title was bestowed on people who made a pilgrimage to Jerusalem. Also in the household was Hagop's mother, whom I called Grandmom. I had no memory of my birth parents.

How clearly I remember Pepron. To try to make me love her, she showered me with kisses and hugs and was always pushing my face into her large soft breasts. Rocking back and forth she'd chant, *seeroum, seeroum,* which means "my dear one." The rough wool of her dress against my face made my skin itch and I had a hard time catching my breath.

Pepron was determined to erase any memory I had of my brothers and sisters. She would sit me down and shout, "I am your mother, you have no one else!"

I cried myself to sleep every night. My daily crying upset Pepron. She'd beat me with her hairbrush and shout, "Stop crying. Forget your family! We are your family now and you will love us."

She beat me every day for a long time. I was five years old. It was hard for me to understand why I should love her when she was so mean to me. I was just a child, but I couldn't help but wonder how anyone could love a person who beat her. As the years passed, I cried less and less and learned to love her more and more.

Pepron was very jealous of anyone who might make me share my love for her. She had no children of her own, and she was afraid of losing me. It was not easy for her because a childless woman in Amasia was looked upon as useless. All the men, including her husband, believed that a woman who does not bear children is like a tree that does not bear fruit — neither one worthy of being kept. Raising me made her feel important, like the other women in town who had children.

Once, as we walked down the street together, some women came up to Pepron and said, "How lucky you are to have found a child that looks so much like you."

Pepron got red in the face. She nudged the woman roughly, and said, "Hush, the child might hear you."

I didn't know I was the child they were talking about.

Our house in Amasia was on a wide, unpaved street. In spite of this, there was very little dust. Many years of horses' hooves pounding rocks and stones into the soft red clay had created a hard surface. Along our street, there were two-story, flat-roofed houses attached to each other. Each house had its own garden and courtyard. In the center of our courtyard we had a large mulberry tree with the sweetest mulberries I ever tasted. I would lie under the thick branches and reach up for handfuls of soft berries. Sometimes they fell off the branches onto my face and eyes. The cool, sweet juice ran down my cheeks into my ears. As the late afternoon sun filtered through the dark green swaying leaves, warming my face and arms, I believed with all my heart that my world would never change. Nothing bad could ever happen to me.

The second floor of our house was the attic where I loved to escape and play make-believe. My friends, Satnig and Tseghag, who lived next door, came over every day after school, and the three of us would climb up to the attic and dress dolls. Such crazy stories we told each other! When the sounds of our laughter and giggles reached Pepron downstairs, she'd poke the ceiling with her broom handle and scold us about the noise.

"Don't you have anything better to do than waste time

talking to dolls?" she'd say. "Come, I have some chores to keep you busy. Life is not just play, you know."

Why isn't it? I thought.

One very big kerosene oil lamp lit up the large room on the first floor of our house. At one end of the room was our living area and at the other end was a fair-sized bedroom with curtains separating my sleeping space from Pepron and Hagop's. Grandmom slept next to me.

Every night we rolled out our *doshegs* to sleep on. By day they were stored in a tall wooden pantry with double doors. On one wall of the living space was our *sadir*. This sofa was our main sitting area with several small pull-up chairs. The *sadir* was always draped with a very fine hand woven rug. The floors, too, were covered with thick, colorful, fine-quality rugs. In the winter, to keep the wind from seeping in through the cracks around the windows, Pepron hung some thick rugs of a lesser quality.

Next to this living space we had our kitchen-dining area. The *toneer,* on the far side of the room, served as our oven and cooktop and was where we cooked all our meals. This *toneer* also warmed our house on cold winter days. Because matches were expensive and not easy to get, we kept the fire going day and night.

Pepron rose early and gently poked and blew on the glowing ashes to ignite a fresh flame. Then she added some dry sticks and heavy logs of slow burning walnut. If our wood supply was low, she added some dried cow dung which we called *geshoud.*

Pepron kept a brass bucket filled with walnut shells next to the blaze and from time to time she'd throw in a handful or two. The glowing walnut shells produced a sweet, nutty smell that stuck to the furniture and walls of our small house. When I smell walnuts today, I think of that room and its sweet smell.

After the fire was crackling hot, Pepron placed a heavy, round black iron plate over the top of the *toneer*. This became the cooktop for the small copper pans she used to fry vegetables and small meats. Pepron mixed lamb chunks with tomatoes, vegetables, and bulgur. Then she added some water to the large iron pot and pushed it deep into the ashes. This stew simmered all day without stirring. By late afternoon when Papa came home from work dinner was ready.

Below the first floor was our *maghazan*. The walls of this basement were lined with rows and rows of *ambars*. Each bin was filled to the brim with wheat, bulgur, lentils, and chickpeas. *Basterma,* or dried, cured beef, and *soujouk,* or sausage, filled other tubs. *Booduks* of cheese in brine and tubs of different jams and olives were lined up on the shelves.

My favorite after-school snack was *vishneh* over hot freshly baked bread. The cool cranberry jam melted and filled all the cracks of the warm crusty bread. The spaces between my teeth oozed jelly and my tongue sloshed in the thick paste.

The temperature in our *maghazan* was always cool, even in the dead of summer. When Papa came home from work on a hot day, he went right down and cracked open a melon that was cooling in the fresh spring that ran beneath our basement.

"Aah," he'd say, as he put his feet up and let the sweet flavor of the melon roll around in his mouth.

"Come, Ester. Have some watermelon with me." Then he'd cut a piece for me and together we'd sit quietly enjoying the space and time together.

Soon, Pepron's harsh voice would shout, "Come, come! Dinner is ready. What's going on down there? Where is everyone?"

In the winter, when frost and freezing conditions covered the countryside, our basement felt the same as it did in the summer. I always wondered, *how did the* maghazan *stay cool in the summer and warm in winter?*

Across the street from our house was a canal and directly opposite our front door was a narrow footbridge that led to the house of Bedros Effendi. This Turkish man and his wife, Herrouh, and their three sons lived in a very big stone house. The first floor was used as a silk factory. The family lived on the second and third floors. On warm summer evenings our families sat on the footbridge, where it was much cooler, talking and drinking coffee for many hours.

During this time the women sat huddled on one side and the men talked politics on the other. We children played a sliding game on the banks of the canal. The lucky ones caught themselves before they reached the shallow water. The losers got wet. This canal served as a water duct in times of heavy rain. Sometimes the water was so high it swept away chickens and small animals along the walk above. My friends and I would laugh and laugh at the sight of those poor creatures sliding, clucking, and scrambling as they desperately tried to grasp the walls of the steep bank to avoid crashing into the raging water below.

My father sold Bedros Effendi leaves from our mulberry *(toot)* tree to cover the silkworm beds. Layers upon layers of leaves would be spread over the worms. As the worms ate through the leaves, they spit out tiny threads and made a cocoon. It was from the cocoon that the silk was harvested.

September was harvest time. This was a special time of year. There were many parties and celebrations. Large vats of *keshgeg* stood like monuments in the street as they bubbled and gurgled over the slow-cooking coals. This mixture of lamb and wheat simmered all day. Musicians played the *davoul* and *zourna,* and all the local townspeople joined in the festivities. I danced and danced. When I was tired, I stopped and had a bowl of the hot *keshgeg,* which was served with melted butter poured on top. Some sour *tourshee* was served as an accompaniment. The spicy sour pickles tasted so good with the *keshgeg.* Oh, what fun we had.

The house attached to our house on the right was owned by Papa's cousin, Dickran Ahronian. He had the only bakeshop oven in our section of town, so all the neighbors prepared their dough at home and brought it to cousin Dickran's oven to bake. Saturday and Wednesday were baking days. Uncle Dickran charged twenty "coins" for this service.

The air on Saturday and Wednesday was filled with the wonderful aroma of freshly baked bread. We had a small oven in our house but most of our neighbors didn't. In the summer even those who had ovens chose to take their dough to the baker because they didn't want to suffer the heat thrown off by the ovens. Uncle Dickran baked our bread for free. We saved twenty coins each time.

On Sundays, we always had a special dinner of pilaf and *karouma.* The roasted lamb had been butchered in the summer and stored in our basement for the winter. We always had more than enough to last through the cold winter. As needed, Pepron sliced off chunks of meat covered with fat and browned them over the fire. We'd huddle near the warmth of the *toneer* and smell the fragrance of the sizzling lamb. As the lamb roasted in the copper skillet, little bubbles of fat exploded and spat out at me. I would lean in closer for more aroma and warmth. Then, without warning, Pepron would pull me back by my ear.

"Silly girl, your hair will catch fire," she'd say.

I'd sit back patiently and wait until she was busy with

something else, then I'd lean in even closer, daring the fire to get me.

On special occasions or holidays, we had chicken. Perhaps a wedding, a visiting official, a funeral, Christmas, or Easter called for the serving of this special bird. Serving chicken was the highest honor one could pay to a guest, for to kill a chicken that was laying eggs was a display of extreme generosity toward a guest. We rarely had chicken.

When company came to our house, Pepron took special care preparing the meal. She'd cook bulgur pilaf, green beans with onions and tomatoes, and sweet flaky pastry filled with walnuts and honey for dessert. Thick black coffee sweetened with rose water completed the meal.

On these nights the men would play cards after dinner, a game called *scambeel*. We children played word games under the card tables. The women gathered in another section of the room and told stories and read coffee cups. Pepron was a good cup reader. After each woman had finished her coffee, she turned the cup upside down on its saucer. Next the women turned their cups clockwise three times and tapped the bottom once. After the cup cooled, Pepron lifted the cup off the saucer. If the cup stuck to the plate, everyone oohed and aahed, for this meant good luck for the receiver of the reading. The women leaned forward on their elbows, quietly listening to Pepron's predictions.

"You will receive a letter from a stranger," Pepron said to one.

To another, she said, "You will be going on a long voyage."

To still another, she said, "Someone from far away will be visiting you soon." These were Pepron's stock answers. It really didn't matter much what she said because all of these prophecies eventually happened to most of the women anyway, and it was all in good fun.

On cold nights, we children huddled next to the fire and slept until it was time for our company to leave. I never liked to visit our neighbor's house in winter because it was so awful to have to wake up and walk home through the snow and cold. On those nights, we returned home to our cold beds with our teeth chattering. I was always happiest when it was our turn to entertain.

Every morning, Pepron rose early, stoked the fire, and prepared breakfast. Hot milk, olives, cheese, and *choreg*. Amasia *choreg* is well known because it is different than the *choreg* in other provinces. Most *choreg* is made with a mixture of flour, warm water, yeast, salt, eggs, and milk. This mixture, when left to rise, doubles in size; it is then shaped into small balls, baked, and served warm.

Amasia *choreg* has the same ingredients but it is taken one step farther. The dough is rolled out in the shape of a large circle, then butter, oil, and a mixture of finely chopped walnuts is spread over the surface. The circle is then cut into four wedges. Each wedge is laid one upon the other, rolled up into a log, then twisted into a fat rope shape, and baked. There is nothing as sweet as the smell of walnut bread baking.

After breakfast, Pepron milked the two cows in our courtyard. These cows provided all the milk we needed. We also kept three lambs in the courtyard in addition to the meat stored in the basement. Though Papa was in the meat business we kept these courtyard lambs for our personal food supply.

Sometimes, while Pepron was busy with her morning chores, she'd send me on errands. She was very strict.

She'd spit on a rock and say to me, "You get back before this dries or I'll beat you."

I'd run as fast as I could to the address she had given me. One day, rushing back, I got caught in a bunch of cows returning home with a shepherd. Someone was building a house and had left some large piles of wood resting along the wall. I hid behind the wood and luckily missed being run over by the herd. It seemed forever before the herd passed. I stood up, brushed off my skirt, and hurried home. I was very late. Oh boy, was Pepron mad! She grabbed my earlobe and pulled it down hard. I told her I was almost killed by the herd of cattle. She let go of my ear, happy to learn that I had saved myself. After her initial joy, she turned and beat me soundly. Almost getting killed was no excuse for lateness, according to Pepron.

Hajji Hagop, my stepfather, was the town's bookkeeper and accountant. He kept the books for the butcher shop which he owned with his brother, Garabed, and close friend, Katchig. He also kept the records for most of the other shopkeepers in town.

Papa's one foot was lame and he walked with a limp. Grandmom told me it was the result of a beating he got as a young boy by some Turks who were mad because he tried to stop them from robbing another Armenian boy. While they were beating Papa, they saw another group to rob. They quickly tied Papa, with his own belt, to the bridge railing and rushed off to attack the others. Luckily some ladies on their way to the baths set Papa free. His injured leg never fully healed. He made many trips to doctors in Marsovan in search of a cure, but his leg was never the same.

Every night, Grandmom bathed Papa's leg in warm water. The weepy raw surface was always bloody. Some layers of yellow scum formed at the edges. Grandmom gently peeled them off one by one. She spread some green ointment over the wound before she slowly and carefully wrapped the leg. I watched her do this every day.

Papa's brother, Garabed, served as the sales clerk in the

shop and Katchig did all the slaughtering and butchering. The other men in the community looked up to Papa as their elder statesman and took his advice on business matters. Almost nightly, someone would visit our house to ask his opinion and advice about this or that.

One afternoon, Pepron accused me of taking her hand mirror. It was a beautiful, silver, carved mirror that always lay on her dressing table. I said I did not have it and begged her to believe me.

"No, no," she said, "you have it, I know."

I sank into a corner of the room and cried.

She overturned everything in sight. When she came to my *zairee* she screamed, "Aha." She shoved her hand into my school bag and came up with the mirror. I turned stone cold. I could not believe my eyes. She must have planted it for, as God is my witness, I did not take it.

"I knew it," she screamed, and beat me.

I cried myself to sleep and prayed, "Please, God, tell me why she is doing this to me?" I got no answer.

After these angry beatings a sense of calm came over Pepron. It was as though she needed to hurt me in order to love me. Fear of Pepron's wrath made me try harder to please her.

Just outside the town was an old castle on top of a ledge that overlooked the city. From a secret spot high on this hill I could see the winding river below me, the Marsovan Plains, and the surrounding mountains miles away. In either direction, as far as my eyes could see, there were miles and miles of beautiful gardens and orchards.

From my lookout point, I watched the waterwheels turning slowly within the city limits. The gentle tipping of the water drummed a steady beat, constant and comforting. I sometimes listened for hours. The slow, even sound reminded me of the Gregorian chants I heard in church every Sunday. These water wheels provided Amasia with the water it needed to feed the bushy landscape.

Everywhere my eye rested, I saw fruits and flowers blooming. On these days, I picked flowers for Pepron. Her favorite and mine was a bright yellow color with long, thin, spine-shaped leaves. It smelled as sweet as honeysuckle.

Alone on the peak I'd toss my books in the air and twirl my body round and round. My long brown hair flew out around my head in the gentle breeze. Dreams of traveling beyond the mountains somewhere in the distance flooded my brain.

Within my sight, only a day's journey away by foot, was the gorge formed by the Yeçil River. Just past it in the distant valley of the Lycus, I could see the faint mountaintops of a place that was once home to legendary Amazonian women.

One evening, as we sat by the fire, Grandmom told me the legend of the Amazons.

She said, "The ancient Greeks believed there was a race of female warriors living near the Black Sea called the Amazons. Their name," she said, "came from a Greek word meaning without a breast, because the girls had their right breasts burnt off so they could draw the bow better. These women were the breadwinners of the family. They worked as laborers in the fields, and because of their great skills, they were the masters and their men were looked upon as slaves."

Oh, how I wished I had lived in that time. In my town the men were so bossy and women were powerless in any matters of importance. Drawn to this place of Amazonian women, I'd strain my neck and lean far out over the ledge hoping to see one. I never saw any.

Grandmom also told me that a long time ago, German

colonists had come to Amasia. But the Germans were not able to maintain their nationality. They married Armenian girls, took up the Armenian traditions of their wives, and lost their German culture. A good example of this was my father's cousin, Bedros Effendi, who married a German girl named Gretel. Gretel learned the Armenian language and customs and never mentioned her German background. For a long time, I believed she was Armenian. Gretel had pale skin, deep set blue eyes, and long flowing blond hair. I was sure that Gretel was an angel sent from heaven.

If I leaned far over the castle wall on the western side of the mountain, I could see a field gun wedged into the side of the mountain. During the thirty days of Ramadan, when Muslims fasted for thirty days, this field gun sounded nightly at sunset, telling the Muslims that it was time to break the day's fast. This was such an important moment that the government did not allow anyone to sound the gun who was not one of their officials. Papa told me that he often saw Muslims with their forks and knives held in midair, waiting for the sound that allowed them to eat.

One day Papa asked me, "Did I ever tell you the story of Ramadan and the New Moon?"

"No, Papa," I answered.

Papa started. "One year, the Mohammedan authorities in Constantinople sent word throughout the land that the new moon had just been seen, and that the Feast of Bairam should begin. When the Muslims in Amasia got this telegram, they too were anxious to begin the Feast but could see no new moon anywhere. So no one believed. The people of Amasia sent word to Constantinople that they would wait and see the new moon for themselves."

As Papa told me this story he laughed then said, "You see,

my child, the government is not always right. You must trust what your eyes tell you and not follow blindly like cattle. I hope you are never fooled by the government."

"I won't be fooled, Papa."

Papa looked at me funny, the way people do when they don't believe what you are saying, then he reached over and mussed my hair.

I often watched the Turkish men praying five times a day. Each time before they bowed in prayer they washed their hands, feet, and behind their ears. Because only the men were allowed in the mosque, the women had to pray at home. During these prayers Muslims all over the world were bowed on their prayer rugs at the same time facing Mecca. I was happy we Christians only prayed together on Sundays; that was enough for me.

Sometimes, after school, my friends and I went to the Mirror Tomb, which was a large, carved rock monument that stood in a gorge above the town. This tomb was cut into the face of the rock looking eastward across the river. We climbed the eight steps to the narrow ledge alongside the high arched entryway very carefully. The outside walls of the arch of the tomb were so highly polished they looked like mirrors. We played among the large stone monuments of earlier kings and queens.

As I walked through the ruins, I pretended I was a queen, strutting, stopping, gazing, and whispering orders to my invisible servants. Oh, what fun my friends and I had running around the arch hiding from each other. Then, we'd stop and scream because we'd bumped into cloudy, scary faces on the mirrored surface that were our very own reflections.

Before heading home, we sat, ate our snacks of olives, cheese, and bread, and rested in the shade of the huge walnut trees that stood on both sides of the tomb. We talked about the kings and queens who had walked on these grounds hundreds of years before. We bowed to each other and pretended we were royalty.

On one of these trips my friends and I heard the faint tinkle of bells. Looking to see where the sound was coming from, we saw a long row of black and white goats coming along the narrow path below us. Each goat had a bell around its neck. The bells were smaller than the size of an egg but rang out in sharp tones. The gentle ringing of the bells below us sounded like the rustle of wind rushing through trees. As the caravan came closer, we saw that the goats were being led by a goatherd and his dog.

Leaning over the ledge, we called to the goatherd, "Do you know a shortcut back to Amasia?"

"Sure, little ones," he said. "Just let me come around this bend and I'll tell you. It isn't often I get to talk to people. I am mostly alone with my goats."

He sat down on a fallen tree trunk, filled his pipe slowly, and started his tale from ancient times.

"There once was a goatherd by the name of Davut. You children from town may find it hard to understand this country tale but I will tell you anyway."

This sounded like it was going to be a long story. I found a comfortable spot on a soft patch of grass. I plumped up my sweater as a pillow, tucked it under my head, and listened to the goatherd's tale.

"We Kurds live all our lives with our animals and we become very close to them. When a favorite dog or sheep dies, it makes us sad just like when a family member dies. Our animals are part of our lives and we nurse them as though they are our children."

That is why Davut, the goatherd, mourned the death of his pet bear.

Davut had killed many bears among these rocks. He also knew that bears feel very strongly about their young. One day Davut came up against a mother bear. He shot at her as she slept. She wakened and looked for something to throw. Not finding a big enough rock, she picked up her little cub to throw it at him. Davut shot again, this time the bullet went right into the mother's mouth. The tiny cub lay at his dead mother's feet.

Davut cradled the cub up in his arms and took it home. He gave her to one of his dogs to nurse. The dog raised the bear as one of her puppies. His children enjoyed the cub and very often they all tussled around the yard together — dogs, bear, and children. They named the baby bear Mokhanatka. The cub climbed the fruit trees and ate fruit all day long. One day the cub fell out of the tree and broke his leg. Davut set the leg and nursed her back to health. From then on, he called her Lame Mokhanatka.

One spring, several years later, Lame Mokhanatka was sad and gloomy. She climbed to the top of the hill near Davut's house and sniffed the air. She could feel the nearness of other bears. She whined. One evening as Davut walked with her she stopped looked at him, and then looked at the bears over the ridge. Then she slowly walked toward the bears. Before she left, she turned back and licked his hands and howled sadly. Davut understood that she had to leave him. He let her go.

Years later, Davut was asleep in the forest when a giant bear came rushing toward him. He reached for his gun but it was not where he had left it, "Allah," he prayed, "please help me." As the bear came closer, he saw that it limped. Could it be? Yes, it was his dear Lame Mokhanatka. She stopped before him and rolled on the ground in joy as she had done so many times in the past.

Then the bear hurried over to some rocks and brought Davut his gun. The bear was afraid he would not recognize her so she had hidden his gun. Then she motioned for Davut to follow her. He followed Lame Mokhanatka to the edge of a steep cliff. The bear laid down flat and watched something below. Davut leaned down and looked over the edge. A short distance down the incline was a cave, and asleep across the entrance was a full-grown tiger. He took his gun, aimed, and pulled the trigger. The tiger was shot dead. Then Davut started to skin the cat. He was very excited because there had only been one other tiger killed in that region before by the famous Armenian hunter, Akop.

Out of the corner of his eye, Davut saw Lame Mokhanatka gathering tiny bones marked with tiger bites. The bones were scattered about the inside of the cave. Two little heads, thin legs, small hairy paws. She was gathering them in a heap. Davut then knew that the tiger had eaten Lame Mokhanatka's cubs. She could not kill the tiger herself so she came for Davut. The bear scraped some dirt and leaves together and covered the little bones. Then Lame Mokhanatka looked at Davut one more time before she turned and left. He never saw her again."

The goatherd turned to us and said, "Well, little ones, did you ever hear such a tale?"

We stared at each other and shook our heads.

"No, we have never heard such a tale," we said.

We reminded him that he was going to tell us about a shortcut back to town. He scratched the back of his neck, thought for a moment, then told us a route that we all knew was wrong.

After we walked away, Hasmig said, "Hah, he's not so

THREE

THE BRIDE HAS NO UNDERWEAR ON

MARGARET — MAY 1998

"Limonium," the florist had said, watching me finger the wispy leaves as she gently placed them in the narrow cobalt blue glass vase. I placed the bouquet on the table that separated Mother's bed from her roommate's.

Mother leaned over, "Look, the leaves on these flowers are so thin you could blow them right off. My family and I were like these leaves, thin, few, and separated the day we filled our wagon and left Amasia."

Then she turned to me, her eyes flashing with excitement, and exclaimed, "You know, my friend Mary covers me up at night. She helps me go to the bathroom, too. I'm lucky to have her for a roommate."

Yes, Mother has always been lucky in her life. But I wondered, was it luck? Or did she deliberately promote generous behavior from those around her by creating a soft, noncombative attitude toward them?

Mary watched us closely. "You know I'm an old lady too. Who knows who'll go first? It's not easy for me to help your mother, I need help myself."

"I've brought you both some perfume," I said, reaching into my tote bag.

Mother smelled the open bottle I handed her, "Hmmmmm, that smells nice."

I dabbed some behind her ears and on her wrists.

"Oh boy, Ester, now the men will be after you," Mary quipped. "You know your Mother had more than one husband. I never had any."

"Yes, I know," I said.

Then I leaned over to Mother, "Remember Shamil?"

"Who . . . who's Shamil?" Mary shouted, overhearing my whisper.

"He was her Turkish husband."

Mother nudged my arm, pressed her lips to my ear, and whispered, "We don't have to tell her everything. Besides, I couldn't help that marriage. I was taken by that Turk. I had no choice."

Mother punched the air, exemplifying toughness when she said "that Turk."

"It's time for lunch," an aide announced loudly. Mother was only too happy for the interruption. We headed for the elevator to the dining hall.

Reaching the dining hall, which was located in the basement of the building, was an arduous task. Slow-moving residents lined up and waited on the second and third floors for the elevator to take them down. The elevator finally arrived and we moved into the cramped space. I didn't feel comfortable, trapped among walkers and wheelchairs. Neither did Mother.

"Why is it taking so long to get there?" Mother asked.

"It's a slow elevator," I said, turning my head to the wall so she could not see my tears.

A gentle hand touched my face. It belonged to the elegant elderly lady on my right.

"My daughter cries like you when she visits me. Don't worry," she said. "It's harder on you than it is on us. Your mother is safe here. You must not let her see you cry."

I wrapped my arms around this friendly stranger.

"Thank you," she said. "It isn't often we get hugged. Of course our children hug us when they visit, but they have busy lives. They don't come often."

I sat Mother down at a table near the door of the dining hall and secured the bib, set at each place, around her neck with the plastic side facing out. Mother didn't say a word but seconds later she took it off and put the cotton side out. Mother's keen sense of adaptation was still intact.

Later, back in her room, Mother said, "I want to go home."

Her irises darted from side to side. Only when she blinked her eyes did I escape their piercing glare.

Once again I explained, "But Mother, if you fall at home it might be hours before someone finds you."

Her voice broke. I rubbed her face gently with the back of my fingers.

"Are you crying?" I whispered.

"No," she lied.

Mother looked out the window, shrugged her shoulders and said, "You know, I've had some narrow escapes in my life."

This was her old habit of deftly shifting from a tragic subject to a funny one, as if I wouldn't notice. I followed her lead and said,

"I know, Mother, I remember the stories you told me about your life in Amasia before the Turks attacked."

"Did I ever tell you about the time I tricked some Turkish women on the road?"

"No, you didn't."

Mother was eager to tell me stories as they popped into her head.

"Well, it happened during the time I lived in Sivas. I was alone one morning, on my way to the market to sell bread, when four Turkish women blocked my path. They shouted, 'Here comes giavour kuzzuh.' They surrounded me and swung their walking sticks down on my head. But I was too fast for them. I quickly ducked down and they hit each other with the sticks. This stunned them. They stopped, looked at each other, and then at me. Before they figured out what had happened, I hitched up my skirt and ran down the road. I never looked back."

Mother laughed as she told this story. She leaned back in her chair, quite pleased with the memory of her antics.

"I can still see their faces. They were surprised by my getaway. Hah, that was a good day."

I scribbled our conversation in my journal. Soon I noticed Mother watching me intently.

"Write, write," she said in rapid succession. "Write, the bride has no underwear on."

"What, what did you say?" I asked.

"In the old country there's a story about the man who asked his newly married daughter-in-law to write a letter for him. 'What shall I write?' the bride asked. He scratched his

head; nothing came to mind. 'Oh just write a note,' he said. Again, she asked, 'What should I write in the note?' 'Hmmm, write the "bride has no underwear on,"' he said. Embarrassed, the bride ran from the room in tears. The father-in-law had planned to embarrass the shy bride and was enjoying a good laugh. Watching you write reminded me of that story."

There was so much more she had to say, and yet, so much seemed shrouded. Her body, bent and broken. My body, bent and broken as I age. Our lives were so different, and yet, we shared the same skin, her cells, my cells, twisted bits of DNA.

In knowing her life, would I better know my own? In preserving her life, would I also be preserving mine? My mother used to can and preserve fruit. Boil the plums, steep the berries in a sugary broth that at once embalmed them and kept their juice. Is this what I am doing here, now that my own children are grown?

Now Mother smiled. She said, "I remember the funny stories the elders told when I was a young girl. Now I am old and I tell them to anyone who will listen. You like my stories; I know because you always listen carefully."

"Yes Mother, I like your stories."

"I had lots of fun when I was a young girl," she said.

"Tell me about those times, Mother. Tell me how it was before the soldiers came."

FOUR

GROWING UP IN AMASIA

ESTER — 1912–1914

In Amasia, there were five churches and two large monasteries. Every Sunday and on holidays we attended church. I went to Sunday school classes and sang in the church choir. I hated singing in the choir because my voice was always a little off-key. I got away with this for a long time before the choirmaster caught me.

"Ester, come up front," he said. "Good, now sing so I can hear you and see you at the same time."

I was awful. The other children laughed and made fun of me. Outside the church after choir practice, I was so mad I pushed and shoved some of them pretty hard. I was tough for a girl. I was happier wrestling with the boys than gossiping with the girls, which is why the girls talked about me behind my back.

One day, a very rich man in our town died, and our choir was asked to sing at the services. Grandmom came into my room and whispered.

"Come, Ester we'll be late for the funeral."

"I'm not going to any old funeral," I said. "They're so awful and depressing. People crying and wailing over the coffin and the heavy smell of incense and flowers makes me want to throw up. I don't have to go, do I?" I pleaded.

Grandmom took my hand, sat me down and said, "No, my dear, you don't have to go. But before I leave you I want to tell you a story about the man who never went to funerals. He felt the same way you do. So when it was time to attend a funeral, he sent one of his shoes with his servant as a symbol of himself. Each time one of his friends died, he sent a shoe instead of attending. One day, as he lay on his deathbed, he told his servant to spread the word around the countryside for his friends to visit him before he died. The next day his servant found a huge pile of shoes outside the front door. His friends did what he had done for many years, they just sent their shoes."

Grandmom won. I went to the funeral with my family and sang my heart out.

My school was three blocks from my house. Every morning I put on a starched white blouse, which Grandmom had ironed the night before, with a gray wool skirt. All the girls wore white and gray. They weren't always the same style but they were the same color. The boys wore long-sleeved white shirts and gray pants. Sometimes it was hard to tell the boys from the girls if they were sitting and you could not see the pant legs.

Our schoolhouse was one giant room with a stage at one end for plays and recitals. There was a section on the second floor where children were put into groups according to their age. The girls were taught to embroider and sew and some cultural history, but the boys were taught addition and subtraction and how to balance account books.

My teacher taught me how to crochet lace borders on pure silk pillowcases to be set aside for my wedding day. Chasedek, my *varbed,* also taught me how to quilt and sew. Our class quilted fabric for the Turkish officers' heavy winter coats. During these quilting classes I often dreamed of Haroutoun, my older brother, the one that Grandmom told me about. Grandmom told me he was an officer in the Turkish Army. I wondered, would this quilted fabric become a coat worn by my brother? I also wondered where he was and if we would ever meet.

At lunchtime, I often ran the short distance to my house to eat sliced sweet onions and jam on warm, fresh bread. This sandwich tasted so good with a glass of cold milk on a hot day. Other days, I carried my lunch to school in a copper pail. I'd eat my lunch under a tree in the schoolyard and dream of faraway places.

One day, during sewing lesson, the devil got into me. I did some crazy sewing. I sewed in an uneven pattern up and down. I did not follow the design that was drawn on the cloth. The girls around me giggled, cheered, and congratulated me for my brave spirit. I wanted to hear more of their cheers so I continued to destroy the delicate pattern with my wild design. Soon, my teacher saw what was going on. She scolded me in front of the whole class. She also made me rip out all the stitches and start the work all over again. It took two long days of undoing the stitches before I could fix the mess. I hate having to do anything over again, even today. It's all because of that terrible sewing lesson.

Every day after school I'd run to Papa's butcher shop,

which was only a short distance from my school. Papa would lift me high in the air and say, "Well now, my little Ester, what did you learn today at school?"

I would talk about how smart I was and how the teacher used my work as an example to the other students.

"Why, only yesterday, Chasedek pointed me out before the whole class and showed everyone my special sewing," I said.

Papa leaned over that day and patted me on the top of my head. "I'm so proud of you," he said, "you will go far, Ester."

I didn't like fooling Papa, but I loved hearing his praise. It was only half a lie anyway because the teacher did talk about me in front of the whole class. That part, at least, was true.

Some days I would sit for hours and watch Papa working on his accounting books. He was so smart. He could add and subtract faster than anyone I knew. He often corrected the accounting mistakes of his friends and gave them advice on money matters. Oh, how proud I was of Papa.

Every afternoon he had my favorite treat, *halvah* with walnuts, ready for me to nibble on. When he finished his work he would carry my books and we'd walk home arm in arm. We made many stops along the way because the neighborhood men always came out of their shops and asked for his wise advice about business matters. The short walk home sometimes lasted an hour because of these visits. I pushed my shoulders up and my chest out as neighbors patted Papa on his back and thanked him for his thoughts. Being with Papa made me feel important.

I was eleven years old when some of our neighbors with eligible sons started sending flowers to our house with invitations of marriage. Pepron, at the same time, was busy filling a large carved wooden chest with linens and tablecloths to be used after my wedding. The chest also held white gowns trimmed with pastel ribbons and yards of fine lace stacked one over the other.

Pinned to the shoulder of my wedding nightgown was a tiny hand-painted blue glass eye. This blue crystal was a symbol of safety from the evil eye. Although this was a pagan custom, left over from earlier times before Christianity, no self-respecting Armenian mother would let her daughter go out without one pinned to her underclothes, especially on her wedding night.

As we walked home from school on March 12th, Papa and I talked about my birthday party that night. It was my twelfth birthday and I was very excited. Pepron had sewn me a new dress with matching shoes for the celebration. There was to be music and sweets and all my friends were invited. Suddenly, I felt a sharp sting on the side of my face. I turned around and put my hand on the painful spot. I was sure some nasty boy had thrown a rock at me; perhaps one of the boys I pushed around after choir practice. I saw no one.

Papa looked down at me and asked what the problem was.

"I think I was hit with a rock," I said.

Papa said, "You have no marks on the outside of your face, Ester. Little girl, I think you have a bad tooth. Perhaps the daily sweet treats have taken their toll. We'd better get home quickly and put some ice on your face."

It wasn't long before my jaw was swollen and red. "We'd better get her to the dentist," Pepron said.

"No, no, please, it will go away, don't make me go to the dentist, he'll dig it out with a hatchet. I don't want to miss my party."

"Don't worry, it will not hurt. You'll be back in plenty of time for the party," Pepron said.

Well, not quite. Mr. Checkegian, the town dentist, was big and fat. His black hair fell in sweaty curls over his forehead and ran into his thick eyebrows. The hair was so thick that it came down over his eyelids and hid his eyes.

He pulled and yanked my jaw. My head sank deeper into his lap. The tooth broke. He picked up a thick metal prong, which looked just like the one the blacksmith used on his horses. He yanked again and again with my head bobbing in his lap from side to side. His belly covered my face. I could hardly breathe. When this didn't work he stuck my head between his legs. With his fat belly pushed against my nose he dug out the infected tooth. Then he shoved his face close to mine to get a better look. The smell of garlic poured from his mouth. I fainted.

When I opened my eyes, I was home in bed. I could hear my friends in the other room enjoying my birthday party. There I sat in my bed with a hot towel wrapped around my swollen red face. My friends brought me presents and took turns sitting on the edge of my *yorghan*. They ate and drank and played games. I was too weak to open my presents. It was days before the swelling went down.

But I was luckier than my friend Seta, who had a toothache like mine, but instead of pulling her tooth they stuck black, slimy leeches all over her face. Yes, I was lucky they only pulled my tooth.

Not many of the villagers in my town had an *aikee*, a summer house built in the orchards. Our family did. When summer came we went to our *aikee*. The house was a simple wooden cottage. There was one very large room, and a few windows to let in the summer breeze. There was a flat roof where we often slept to escape the hot summer nights. A beautiful open porch wrapped around the front of the house where we gathered in the evening and played games. We had fruit trees, grapevines, and tree houses to play in.

I had my own horse, which I named Aragats. Grandmom told me that Aragats was the name of an old volcano in the northwest corner of Armenia. Aragats was snow white and twelve hands high. I rode him only during the summers at our *aikee*. The workers took care of him through the winter, as we had no room at our house.

There was a deep river that ran through our *aikee* and on hot dry days my friends and I would swim in the clear cool water. I could see my feet in the mud and the passing fish as I walked slowly to the deeper water. One day as I walked along the grassy edge Pepron shoved me into the deep water. She was a strong swimmer and enjoyed pushing me below the surface. As I coughed and tried to get air, she'd shove me down again and again.

Then she'd laugh and say, "This lesson will make you a better swimmer, Ester."

Sure, I thought, if I lived through the lessons. To get away from her, I'd race to the other side of the river where I could watch some teenage boys diving off a steep waterfall. The boys tied large gourds with ropes under their arms to keep them afloat. I wanted to do this too, but this activity was only for the boys. On those days I hated being a girl.

From a secret hiding place, behind some trees, my friends and I watched the boys swim naked under the waterfall. The boys pretended they didn't know we were watching but we knew they knew. Seeing the naked boys gave me a funny feeling in the bottom of my stomach.

"Hey, Ester, your face is red," said a friend.

"No, it's not," I said, and pushed her off her rock into the water.

Our *aikee* was called the chay-bashi, the name given the orchard with the highest quality grapes. I wasn't allowed to pick the grapes because this job was only for the older men in the family. The heat from the sun was so hot the women and children stayed indoors.

Harvest time was an exciting time in our household. Baskets of ripe grapes were brought to our house and taken straight to the basement where they were dumped into a large, eight-foot round *senavat*. The adults carefully washed their feet and pressed the grapes in the tub with a stomping motion. In the bottom half of the *senavat* there were holes where the grape juice ran out into large vats. The white grape juice was the color of weak tea. This was the first pressing.

The leftover juice from this pressing was put into new clean pottery jars to ferment. Pepron tested the bubbling liquid after several days. To do this she held a candle to the top of the open jar. If the candle went out the process was complete and the *oghee* was ready. She kept the windows closed so the aroma would not filter outside. If the Turkish officers smelled the alcohol they would charge a large whiskey tax. Musicians played in the streets outside to distract the Turkish neighbors. The Turkish officers suspected nothing because in the summer there was often music in the streets.

Once, when I was six years old, Papa gathered me up and lowered me into the tub when he thought Pepron wasn't looking. I was so excited I could hear my heart jumping in my chest. Papa put my tiny hands on the sides of the tub and told me to hold tight.

"Jump, Ester," he said. "Jump high."

Oh, how exciting! I could feel the grapes squish between my little toes. They felt cold, wet, and slippery and I squealed with joy. Pepron pretended not to see and allowed the activity to go on for a short while before she scolded Papa with tales about children slipping into the brine and drowning.

"What's the matter with you? Have you no concern for her welfare? Life is not fun and games," she'd moan. "We must set a good example for Ester."

Papa listened to her outburst, then, shyly looking down, he lifted me out of the tub, wiped my feet, and gave me a secret smile.

I remember when I was eleven, my friend Verkineh and I were told to deliver a jar of wine to my uncle down the street. We were never allowed to drink wine but this day the devil got into me.

I said to Verkineh, "Come on, let's taste it."

"Oh no," she said, "we'll be in big trouble if we get caught."

"Don't be silly," I said, "No one will know. Here, try some."

She drank half a glass and said, "Ummmm, that sure does taste good." I had some too. It was sweet, cool, and refreshing after a long day in the hot sun.

"Let's have some more," I said.

"Sure," said Verkineh, "let's have lots more."

Well, the room started spinning and the floor met the ceiling. We giggled and laughed about this great discovery of ours. The next thing I remember was Pepron shaking me and dragging me off to bed. Pepron sent Verkineh home and promised to report what we had done to her mother. The next morning I could not lift my head off the pillow. My first hangover.

Sometimes there were long periods of no rain during the summer. Although irrigation was the main source of water for the orchards, it was always a happy day when rain gave the fields a good drenching. During the dry spells the women gathered together and prayed for rain. They baked a mixture of flour and water into hard, flat, dry bread. Each woman took a square of this bread and stood at the river's edge. Loud prayers filled the air as the women threw the bread upon the water. I became a believer one afternoon when, after lots of chanting and bread throwing, the clouds burst open and sheets of rain came crashing down.

When the time came for us to leave the *aikee* — about late August — my friends and I gathered together and cried and moaned about how we didn't want to leave this happy place. Returning to the city meant summer was over. No more fun-filled days. The serious business of school was around the corner.

Holidays in Amasia were always special to me. My favorite holiday was *Vartevar:* a day in July when water tricks were allowed. It was a day like April Fool's Day, except all the pranks involved water. My friends and I filled cups with water and waited on the rooftop for people to pass by. Then, at just the right moment, we'd flip the water cups and spray the unsuspecting victims. School was closed on this day and parents allowed all sorts of misbehavior that they didn't allow other times. Many of our days were filled with chores and study, so we couldn't wait for *Vartevar* to come each year.

Just after my twelfth birthday I felt a sharp pain in my lower belly. It was *Vartevar* and I didn't want to tell anyone because they might tell Pepron and she would surely put those slimy leeches on me. My friends and I were on the roof with our water cups ready when I sank to the ground. I was having so much fun I had paid no attention to the pain until it became so bad that I doubled over.

"Look, look!" Satenig said, "Your underpants have blood on them."

Oh my God, I must be dying. My friends giggled and snickered. "Didn't your mother ever tell you about *amsagan*?

No, Pepron had never told me about *amsagan*. I hurried home to Pepron. She helped me clean up and showed me how to place cotton rags between my legs to catch the blood. Then she sat me down and explained that I would be bleeding like this once a month.

"But I don't want it," I protested.

Pepron put her arms around my shoulders and said, "You are a woman now and you must behave like one." I didn't understand how one day I was her little girl and the next because of this bloody "thing," I was a woman. I didn't feel any different. I looked at myself in the mirror. Yes, I still looked the same.

Christmas was another of my favorite holidays. All our neighbors visited one another during the Christmas celebration. Each served a delicious sweetbread called *boobegh*. This thin, round cookie with upturned corners held a thin layer of honey and sugar water. Pepron and Grandmom also made our traditional Amasia bread. But at Christmas they placed a coin in the dough before it was baked. Whoever got the piece of bread with the coin would have good luck all year. I always found the coin.

Christmastime was also when the older male relatives gave sparkling gold coins to the children in the family. I loved the feel of the coins tinkling in my hands. One of the last Christmases when we were all together, Pepron had a beautiful tan wool coat made for me. It had ivory embroidery on the shoulders and sleeves. Brown furry tails hung from the fur-trimmed hood. I felt like a princess wearing that soft, warm coat. I still remember it well.

Easter was very special in Amasia. Between Palm Sunday and Easter Sunday, we Gregorian Christians celebrated Christ's story in the church. The Thursday before Easter, the men of the parish dressed up as Christ's disciples and re-enacted the washing of the disciples' feet by Jesus as written in the New Testament. On Friday night, a coffin was carried down the aisle, followed by grieving parishioners mourning the death of Jesus Christ. The smell of incense was so strong it was hard to breathe. Sometimes older women were overcome by the strong fumes and fainted.

At the altar, the priest prepared a marble basin filled with water for the immersing of the cross. The family that donated the largest sum to the church had the honor of plunging the cross into the water and lifting it high in the air. One year, Papa purchased this honor for my cousin, John. Oh, how I wished I was born a boy. Boys got to do all the fun things. John was dressed in a long white brocaded robe trimmed with thick bands of twisted rope made with silver and gold thread. All eyes in the church were upon him as he slowly lowered the cross into the water. At that moment I hated John.

When Easter Sunday arrived, after a week of fasting, mourning, and weeping, the happiness of the resurrection was thrilling. Each year, Pepron made me a new Easter dress. The last dress she sewed for me was peach-colored velvet. I wore peach ribbons in my hair and thin white lace gloves to cover my hands. Perched on my head was a peach-colored hat with matching velvet ribbons and white lace. Attached to the back of the hat, like it was an afterthought, was one large white silk flower. I felt so beautiful that day.

Easter Sunday, like Christmas, was the time to visit other family members. Upon entering the household, the head of the family gave one hard-boiled egg and a gold coin to each child. One year I ate all the eggs as they were given to me. By the time I reached home, I was so sick I had to be put to bed. I was lucky no one mentioned leeches.

Pepron worked for weeks preparing the Easter feast for

our family. For weeks ahead, each time she skinned an onion for a meal she put the skins in a bag on the floor. By Easter, the bag was full and ready for egg coloring. As the eggs boiled with the onion skins, they took on a rich deep orange-red color. The longer the eggs rested in the colored water, the deeper the red.

After the four-hour Easter Sunday service, we all went down to the church hall beneath the chapel. Coffee, *choreg,* *lahmajun,* boiled eggs, a large variety of sweet cakes and fruit pies were set out on long metal tables for the parishioners to purchase. Everyone greeted one another with the phrase *"Soorp Asdvadz,"* Christ has risen. We'd slowly march around the hall carefully looking over the Easter finery worn by our friends and neighbors. It was also a time for families to look for bridegrooms for their daughters and brides for their sons. I made mental notes of the girls in the prettiest dresses and, of course, the handsomest boys.

Bags of hard-boiled eggs to be used in the egg fighting were sold by the dozen. The game of egg fighting was a big event at Easter. Papa always bought me two bags of eggs for the egg fight. To "fight eggs," one boy or girl holds a hard-boiled egg in his or her hand with just the tip showing. The object is to crack your opponent's egg without cracking your own first. We took turns holding our egg while the other player hit our egg with theirs. The person who cracked all the others without cracking his own first won a prize.

Papa taught me how to test eggs by gently tapping the egg against my teeth. A deep sound and vibration would mean a firm solid egg. If there was no sound the egg could be a rock. There were cheaters who sometimes used a colored rock for an egg. One could easily be fooled by this trick, but Papa always had me test for fake eggs. Thanks to Papa, I was never fooled by the cheaters.

There was also a yearly celebration in Amasia called "*dohn.*" It was a time to celebrate one's name. Papa's *dohn* came right after Easter and the party was always held at our house. Relatives and friends came for dinner, coffee, and dessert. Each brought a candle, lit it, and handed it to Papa with the words, *anoonovet dzeranas*. I thought it was silly to tell someone to "grow old with his name." How could one grow old without his name?

The candles were all different sizes and shapes. Each donor searched for the most unusual candle. Each wanted his candle to be the most admired. All the candles were placed on the dining table until the surface seemed to be completely covered. Yet every time another candle arrived, Pepron managed to squeeze it in. Once, a towel caught fire, but Grandmom quickly shoved it into a bucket of water, saving the party and our house.

A short while after my thirteenth birthday, Pepron became ill. They said she had pneumonia. The doctor came every day. I heard Papa and the doctor whispering softly across the room.

"She is going to die," I heard the doctor say before Grandmom pushed me aside.

"No, no," Papa wept loudly.

I didn't want Pepron to die. What would happen to me if she died? I wanted to say something to Papa, but he waved his hand in the air the way he sometimes did when he wanted me to leave him alone. The next day Pepron was dead.

Neighbors came to pay their respects to Papa. There was a ceremony at church before we lowered her into the ground at the cemetery. I cried. Not just for Pepron. I cried for Papa, who looked very sad. I cried for Grandmom, whose shoulders slumped so low it was as though she was carrying the weight of many pounds of grain on her back. Mostly I cried for me. I had come to love Pepron as a mother. Who would scrub my hair at the baths? Who would scold me when I was late returning from errands? I cried day and night. I asked God why I kept losing mothers. Grandmom tried to comfort me, but she was an old woman and didn't understand what I was feeling.

"Hush," she'd say. "You must not cry. It upsets your father."

The house was large and required the work of another able-bodied woman. Papa was lonesome and sad. We didn't talk much. He ate his dinner and went to bed. No stories, no jokes. After a while even the neighbors stayed away to observe his privacy.

After a few months, I noticed that our neighbor, Vartouhi, who lived down the street, was coming over to visit more and more. Her husband had died of typhus five years earlier, and our families were close friends. She also had a seven-year-old son named Arsen. I was not surprised the day Papa told me about his marriage plans.

"Well, what do you think, Ester?"

What do I think? No one ever asked me what I thought.

Before I could think of an answer Papa said, "I knew you would be happy. Arsen will be company for you. You'll see, he will be a big help to you with the chores. You know Grandmom is old and you have much too much work to do.

Papa and Vartouhi had a small ceremony after church services on Sunday, followed by a big dinner for friends and neighbors at our house. In honor of this occasion, we cooked up some of our fattest chickens.

Papa was right. After Vartouhi and Arsen moved in, my life took a different turn. It was nice to have a seven-year-old brother. Arsen and I played games and told each other stories. I liked having someone around that I could give orders to. Best of all, Papa was happy.

Several months later, I woke up coughing and spitting. My head was burning and my throat was so sore I could not talk. The week before, I had some sniffles and a running nose, but I had no fever. Vartouhi and Grandmom quickly changed my sweaty bedclothes and fixed me some hot broth.

"She must rest," Grandmom said. "Vartouhi, you get some water and a knife."

As I drank the water, Grandmom circled my bed with a knife in her hand raised high in the air.

"*Erigah char, guhneega paree, erigah char, guhneega paree.*"

She chanted the same words over and over as she came nearer and nearer. I closed my eyes and thought, *is she going to kill me because I'm so sick? Is Grandmom trying to save me from suffering by killing me before I die? Is she sending me to be with Pepron?*

I may have been out of mind with fever, but I was sure she was saying the words differently each time. The first chant was "husband bad, wife good," the second chant was "wife bad, husband good."

She danced around the room screaming loudly, *"erigah char, guhneega paree, guhneega char, erigah paree."* She circled the air with the knife and moved in closer. I held my breath and waited for the blow.

Suddenly, Grandmom turned red in the face, sputtered and gasped for breath. She jumped around the room like a crazy person. She chanted some more then fell to the floor.

I was frightened. What happened to her? What will happen to me? I was so sick with fever and convulsions I really didn't care very much about either of us. Then, like Lazarus rising from the dead, she rose up, spat on the knife, and stuck it into the dirt floor in a corner of the room.

"There," she said, quite satisfied with her performance. "That will get rid of the evil spirits in your body." Vartouhi cried. Arsen hid in the attic.

Almost immediately, my fever broke. I slept for two days. When I was feeling a little better, I asked Grandmom to explain what had happened.

"Tzakgiss," she said. "Many years ago I made a pilgrimage to Jerusalem and there I obtained my healing hand from an old priest. The chants call up protective spirits that help me bring the illness to myself and away from the person who is ill. Then I transfer the evil to the knife and into the ground safely away from the sick person. In a few days, when you are much better, I will give you my healing hand. This will be my gift to you, dear Ester."

A few days later, true to her word, Grandmom gave me her healing hand. She clasped my right hand tightly in hers and slowly chanted, "I give to you my healing hand." With her eyes closed, she swayed from side to side holding my hand in hers.

We rocked, she chanted, "I give to you my healing hand" over and over. Then, a warm rush ran up my right arm. I looked up at Grandmom. She smiled.

"It is done," she said. "One day you will pass this healing hand to someone you love."

I never told anyone about this gift from Grandmom. I was afraid they would think I was crazy.

Once a week, Vartouhi, Grandmom, and I went to the bathhouse. During these visits to the bathhouse, mothers and grandmothers of boys would come to look over the town's young girls. Each was looking for the best bride for their sons and grandsons. It was a whole-day affair. We packed our lunch and clean fresh clothes in large straw baskets.

After entering a very large marble hall, we paid our fee and proceeded to the main section of the bathhouse. This space was much larger than the entry hall. The walls and floors were covered with shiny white tiles. There were low wooden benches around the room to sit on. Buckets of hot water were brought in by workers to rinse away the soap and layers of dead skin and dirt scrubbed off by the horsehair brushes — *keses*. A shallow trench ran along the floor to catch the dirty water flowing through the halls.

Bathing was not the only thing women did at the bathhouse. As the younger girls played games with marbles and cards, the older women sat in small groups and gossiped. My breasts were starting to show. There was no way I could hide my body in the bathhouse, except to bend my shoulders as far down as I could to hide the ugly things growing above my waist. I undid my braids, hoping my long hair would cover most of my body.

One time, a fat woman wrapped in a very large white sheet came waddling over to us. "Oh, how silky Ester's hair is. Vartouhi, what kind of soap are you using?" she asked.

Vartouhi ignored her. The woman left.

"She's such a fool," Vartouhi said. "We all use the same homemade soap, I have no need to talk with that stupid woman. Come Ester, let's move over to the other side of the room, in case she returns."

I sat down on a low bench and dropped my feet into the warm soapy water that flowed in the narrow trench. Vartouhi scrubbed my body with the *kese* and layers of skin peeled off along with the scum that had built up over a week's time. I think I lost a pound of flesh each week at the bathhouse.

Next, Vartouhi filled her hands with soap, poured warm water over my head and scrubbed my hair. My long hair always got tangled into tight knots. This was the part I hated. While

Vartouhi combed the soap out, Grandmom poured water over my head. Well, combing is what they called it. Yanking and pulling my hair out by the roots is what I called it. They repeated this again and again. With all the pulling and tearing it's a wonder I have any hair left.

Now finished with me, Vartouhi and Grandmom scrubbed themselves while I wandered around the hall looking for my friends. The room was clouded with steam. The smooth tile walls and floor echoed the whispers of the bathers. Ghost-like figures moved slowly around the room wearing only large white flowing sheets. Some women knelt and stepped in large tubs of sweet smelling liquid. The room was hot and stuffy and it was sometimes hard to breathe. I could hear the familiar laughter of my classmates. In the semi-darkness I started to follow the sound toward my friends.

Before I could get away, Vartouhi pinched my arm hard. "Remember, don't sit on any benches unless you put a towel down first."

No further explanation was needed. I knew the story well. Every week, either Grandmom or Vartouhi reminded me about the young girl who sat on a bench and got pregnant. Because men and women used the bathhouse on different days, it was believed that leftover sperm was sitting on the warm bench and wiggled its way into the young girl's body. *Now that's a strong sperm.* I never did believe old wives' tales, but I also never sat directly on the wet benches.

Some days I saw women putting leeches on different parts of their body for pain relief. Once Vartouhi put a leech in my hand.

"Here, Ester, hold this for me." Though I had seen leeches before I had never held one.

I felt a sharp sting like a needle as the leech attached itself to my hand. The black slimy bug hung on my skin.

I shook my hand over and over, but the bug held fast. "Take it off, take it off!" I screamed.

"Oh, stop crying," Vartouhi said. "Someday you may have pain and you will have to have leeches applied."

I secretly vowed never again to tell anyone if I had any pain.

Once, I saw a young girl insert a leech, which was inside of a tiny copper cage-like box, into her vagina. I never asked why she did this and no one offered to tell me.

After an hour or two of sweating and scrubbing, we'd go to the cooling off room. There we put on our clean clothes and had our snacks. Vartouhi usually packed fresh baked *cheoreg* and cheese with fruit. This was the time to see and be seen by the other bathers. We all wore our finest dresses and greeted one another with the phrase, "I wish you a hundred years of clean life, as well as a clean body." Many in the group kissed Grandmom's hand as a sign of respect for her age. Grandmom always smiled sweetly and held out her hand to all.

When I was fourteen years old, I was told that my eighteen-year-old brother Haroutoun was coming for a visit. I was so excited! I thought, *Could it be true, my very own brother looking for me?* Vartouhi told me that he was coming to see if I was well and happy. Whenever I asked Grandmom about my sisters and brothers, the subject was changed and I was hushed. I had so many questions to ask this brother whom I had not seen for years.

The day he was to arrive I dressed slowly, taking special care. I wanted him to like me. I chose a rose-colored dress with deep purple trim and black suede shoes. I brushed my hair for an hour, added a pink ribbon to the long single braid down my back, and waited. Would I remember his face? Haroutoun Minerajian, my only link to the past! My only living relative! I twisted my fingers and bit my lips.

It was Vartouhi who answered the loud knock on the door. Haroutoun stood in the doorframe bathed in an orange glow from the near setting sun. He was tall. He had fine features, dark eyes, and wavy brown hair. He wore a Turkish army uniform covered with medals and shiny gold braids. He entered the room, shook hands with Hagop and Vartouhi, and slowly walked toward me. He stood for a long time, only inches away, and stared at me. Then, with a swift motion, Haroutoun leaned forward, picked me up, and swung me around.

Then he smiled, kissed my forehead, and said, "You look just like Mother."

Vartouhi coughed nervously and nudged Papa to serve the drinks.

I sat very close to Haroutoun and listened as he described his job in the Turkish army. Haroutoun said he learned to speak German while attending a mission school.

"The Turks have aligned themselves with Germany," he continued. "My job as a translator and emissary between the Turks and Germans has become very important."

Haroutoun held both my hands in his and looked deep into my eyes as though he was trying to read my mind. How strange I felt. This young man that I had no memory of filled me with a warm sense of comfort. I would have left with him that minute to go anywhere he said.

He leaned forward and whispered in my ear, "My precious Ester, if you ever need me, I will be there for you."

Vartouhi broke the spell with, "Come now, I have prepared a meal for us. You must be hungry after your long journey."

All I could think was, *What journey? Where had he come from?* I had so many questions to ask but children were expected to be silent. I kept my thoughts to myself.

Haroutoun told Papa and Vartouhi that there was trouble brewing in the land.

He said, "Many Armenians are being hanged daily in other towns. You must be ready to leave at a moment's notice. Make preparations so you can escape quickly, for when the order is given, and it will be soon, there will be little or no advance notice. Do not trust any Turkish friends you may think you have, because they will betray you."

Then he told us a story about two families he knew in a neighboring town who had lived next door to one another for three generations. The Turkish husband said to his Armenian neighbor, "Don't worry, your family and mine have been friends for years. Your children and mine are playmates. Your wife and my wife are best friends. I will not let any of you suffer. I will hone and sharpen my knives every day so that when the order comes, I will slit all of your throats swiftly and cleanly. You and your family will not experience any pain or suffering. This I vow to you, my dear friend."

My mouth dropped open. I could not believe my ears.

"You see," said my brother, "no one will be spared, trust me, I know. I am hearing about Armenians being murdered daily, because I am a high-ranking officer. But even my family will not be spared. I will not be able to help you. I can only warn you to get out. Leaving quickly is the only answer to this madness."

Hagop nudged Vartouhi. She stood up and said, "Please, no more talk of this; you are frightening Ester."

The conversation then changed to more pleasant matters. Soon, Haroutoun rose to leave. We said our good-byes with laughter and hugs and talked about the promise of another visit soon.

Before he went out the door he wrapped his arms around my shoulders. His eyes were wet, he said, "Dear Ester, I will miss you. You'll be fifteen next month. Where have the years gone? Remember, trust no one. Will you promise me this?"

"I promise," I said.

FIVE

THE DAY MY FATHER DIED

MARGARET — JUNE 1998

Mother removed the paper surrounding the tea roses very slowly. "Oh! They're my favorite color," she exclaimed. She lifted the roses toward the picture of her brother Haroutoun that hung on the wall above her bed.

"Look, Haroutoun, Margaret brought me pink roses!"

Then to me she said, "Our neighbor in Amasia had little roses like these in her garden. We didn't. Once in a while she would give me a few. These are so pretty. Umm, and they smell good, too."

Mother's eyes clouded over. "Such lovely little petals. My life in Amasia was like these flowers — beautiful and sweet. I never dreamed it would end."

I was startled when Mother suddenly asked; "Does your husband beat you?"

"Yes," I said, "all the time."

She knew I was kidding, and she responded with "Good, you probably need it."

I helped Mother to the bathroom but not in time. I wiped her bottom and helped her pull up fresh underpants and slacks.

"I used to dress you and now you dress me," she murmured. Then sadly, "I'm sorry I made a mess."

"It's okay, Mother." I could see she was uncomfortable. The indignity of having one's behind wiped, even by one's own child, must be painfully degrading. I sat her on the edge of her bed and massaged her neck, legs and feet with baby oil. As the lotion squished between her toes, Mother giggled.

"Mother, are you ticklish?"

"No," she replied, "my feet are so old they've forgotten how to be ticklish." I pressed my nose against her toes and asked, "Are you ticklish?" Mother laughed.

"See, perhaps you are ticklish," I teased.

"I wish your Papa was here with me," she said. "Maybe he's found a new wife."

"No, I'm sure he's waiting for you in heaven."

"When a man wants a woman he doesn't wait. Your Papa used to say, 'Hatz, boots, arkaioutoon' — bread, vagina, heaven. Now look what you made me say! You are a naughty girl indeed.

"Shamil, the Turk, who took me from the orphanage, cursed my family, my God, my religion, me. Did you know that he cheated on me with other women, too?"

Tapping her forehead with a clenched fist, she said, "Lots of stuff has happened to this head.

"Remember that love is stronger than hate. Your father's

love for me let me grow again. His love was food as water is food for these flowers."

Then she startled me with, "I see your Papa now."

This scared me. "What is he saying?" I asked.

"He says he always wanted a boy but this one, pointing to you, is better than any boy. He says he loves you."

"But you told me that when I was born Papa was so disappointed I wasn't a boy he disgustedly slammed his hand down and left the hospital room."

"Oh, he changed his mind when you were just weeks old. Once you were born he loved you very much. Why, he carried you to Radio City Music Hall on his shoulders to see the Rockettes when you were three years old. What a terrible thing death is," she mumbled.

"Are you afraid of dying?" I asked.

"No, I'm not afraid. I've been so close so many times, one of these days I'm gonna go. No, I'm not afraid. It's sad for those who are left behind, because they are separated from their loved ones.

"When my Papa was taken away in Amasia, I felt so alone. No one understood how I felt. I still miss him today," Mother said.

I understood only too well how she felt, for I, too, felt the same sense of abandonment the day my father died.

I remember it was 6:30 P.M. and Papa had just come home from his job as a drill press operator. It was July 7th and record-breaking heat spread like bubbling lava over the city.

Papa looked pale and clammy after his long bus and subway ride. The five-story climb to our apartment was difficult on a cool day, even for a young person. Papa was fifty-seven.

"Are you hungry, Albert?" Mother asked.

"No, not really. I think I'll just lie down for a little while."

"What?" Mother complained. "My dinner will be spoiled. Come and eat first."

Papa ignored Mother and slowly shuffled across the floor towards the bedroom they shared, as though the weight of the world was on his hunched, sweat-drenched shoulders.

I had been reading in the living room when the paramedics came bounding up the stairs. These strange men wearing white uniforms emblazoned with a Red Cross emblem on the left pocket hurried past me. The stream seemed endless. One pushed a stretcher; another carried oxygen. Then a sweaty guy in a wrinkled brown suit arrived carrying a black satchel. A red and blue food-stained tie hung loosely from his neck. Everyone pushed into the tiny bedroom. I couldn't see Mother, but I recognized her voice. She was crying, "Albert, Albert. Asdvadz eem!"

"Over here with that oxygen," a voice shouted. I pressed my back against the silver painted upright radiator along the far wall of the living room.

During the winter our apartment was the last to get any heat. This radiator I was clinging to was our "bread of life." It was my job to hit the radiator with a large metal spoon, which caused an annoying clanging sound that, hopefully, would wake the superintendent to let him know we were freezing. When he got sick of hearing the din, he fired up the furnace and sent up some heat. I clung to the radiator that day as if it would respond as it did on those cold winter days and make everything all right. I was confused. I was thirteen.

Minutes later, the entourage filed past me again. Only now the stretcher had Papa on it. His naked arm fell off the gurney as he passed me. I reached out for his hand.

"No, little lady, he's dead," a voice said as he flung the lifeless limb back onto the stretcher. "Nothing you can do for him now."

The three-day viewing at the funeral chapel seemed like an eternity. Papa lay in a satin-lined coffin as people stepped up to look at him. They'd say a short prayer, cross themselves, and move on.

We sat in the front row next to Papa. We stared at him most of the day and into the evening as people came and went. Some brought food, which we ate in a small alcove off the viewing room.

Mother cried openly as she greeted visitors.

A neighbor lady warned me, "Margaret, you must not cry. If you do, you will upset your mother."

When I couldn't hold back my tears another minute, a fat lady — smelling of garlic and sweat — shoved my face into her bulbous breasts and stifled my sobs. Every few minutes Mother cried out about the injustice of Papa's dying. I sat quietly twisting a pink handkerchief in my hands, and tried not to cry.

Woodlawn Cemetery in The Bronx sat on a bluff above the highway that led to Van Cortland Park. A grove of trees stood at the top of the hill. The freshly dug grave stuck out in the middle of the worn tombstones. There was a faded canvas tent, some plastic grass and a few folding chairs. It was very still. Someone read in Armenian from the Bible. The priest sang a mournful song for the dead.

I peered into the black hole beneath the coffin. It looked cold, dark, and damp. Papa liked warmth and light. The funeral director gave each of us a red carnation. I clutched it tightly in my fist, waiting for the signal to toss it onto the tall mound of flowers piled high on the casket. After the first flower was tossed I reached over the coffin and gently let go of my flower. The bright red carnation slid down from the pile into the dark space beneath the box. I cried for Papa alone in the dark with only my flower for company. A lone Canada goose waddled by and startled me.

It was around this time that the squid first entered my room. It only came out after all the lights were out and the apartment was quiet. It entered by the window and spread like incoming tide across the room to the door where it rose and hung on a hook, looking down on me. I'd shut my eyes to make the squid go away but I could almost feel it clammy against my skin. Then I'd open my eyes wide and see it hanging on the door waiting for me to move. I stayed very still listening to my heartbeat. My skin was wet and cold. It was a long while before I realized that the moonlight beaming in through the window was creating the shadow I thought was a squid. In the morning the squid silhouetted against the door became my mother's bathrobe hanging on a bent nail on the back of my bedroom door. I was convinced that if Papa were alive the creature would never have appeared.

As a sign of respect for my departed father, and in keeping with the mourning practices of the time, Mother insisted we both wear black for a year. She vowed also to keep the television set turned off for our year of mourning.

After about a month, a neighbor remarked to Mother, "It's too hard on the child. You must try to have a more normal life for Margaret."

Mother turned the television set on after six months. I continued to wear black, although some of my black blouses had white collars.

I was now a high school student in The Bronx. In those

days there was no such thing as a snow day. No matter how deep the snow, I plodded the five blocks to the elevated train that always ran, and reached school pretty much on time. The teachers who had to take a bus or drive usually didn't show up. Classes were held anyway.

On my return home, I'd get off at Tremont Avenue, the stop before mine. It was only three short blocks to a cavernous Catholic church, which in those days was always open. Pressing my knees deep into the soft kneeling pad, I prayed to God to take good care of my Papa. I sat. I knelt. I cried. Then I'd have a conversation with Papa. I told him about my grades, my teachers, my lack of friends, and my non-existent boyfriends. No one asked why I was there. No one asked why I was crying. Before I left I'd light a candle and watch the golden flame slip away into an ugly, floppy blob that was eventually sucked into the fiery recesses of the hot wax.

Then I'd bundle myself up for the long walk home. Only two tokens a day were allotted. I had used them both. I told no one about my daily visits with Papa.

I shook off these memories when Mother woke from her nap, wide-eyed, and said, "You know the night the Turkish soldiers took my Papa away, we had no warning, no notice.

"As they dragged him through the door, he said, 'Don't worry. I promise we'll have breakfast together tomorrow before you go to school.' I never saw him again."

Mother, like me, never had a chance to say goodbye. I was thirteen when I lost my father. Mother was fifteen when she lost hers. We are linked, yes, by cells and skin, twisted bits of DNA; and then this. We are linked by loss.

I was exhausted after this visit and grateful that my son Steven was waiting to drive me home. I climbed into the car, adjusted my seat belt, and pushed the recline button. Steven *was a good driver and I knew I could close my eyes and rest during the two-hour drive to Pennsylvania.*

As we drove over the George Washington Bridge, I noticed the rusted, chipped, weather-beaten metal railings. Soon this metal would be sanded, buffed, painted, and made to look new. If only one could stop the ravages of time. I wondered, did I have my mother's strength? Would I live to be 98? I looked at my aging reflection in the windowpane and then I looked over at Steven. He was handsome, strong, and full of life. He looked so much like his father. I fell asleep.

SIX

SIGNS OF UNREST

ESTER — MAY 1915

In May of 1915, I began to notice a change in the visiting habits of our neighbors. A steady stream of visitors arrived daily. The usual light conversation and joke telling had disappeared. The older men and women talked in whispers behind closed doors. It was as if they were hiding from something outside. If any children entered the room, the adults quickly changed the conversation to the weather or food until the youngsters left. I was fifteen. Old enough to know that something was wrong.

I remember the look on Papa's face as he sat in the corner of the *sadir* holding Vartouhi's hand.

"Haroutoun warned us of the hangings. He said we should

leave Amasia for a safer place and I agree with him. Let's go now before it's too late," Vartouhi said.

Papa put his arm around her, "Now, now, don't be alarmed. I'll know when the time is right. My friend, the Turkish council chief, told me he would allow us plenty of time to sell our belongings and arrange matters about the business in the courts before the trouble."

"But you will never get the chance to settle your matters in a Turkish court of law. You know about *Kurd der vourar.* You know you will never get what's rightfully yours," said Vartouhi.

"What trouble? What's *Kurd der vourar,* Papa?" I asked.

"Oh, nothing to worry your pretty little head about. Little girls should laugh and be gay and leave the worrying to the elders."

Papa did not answer my question.

Grandmom gave me a look that meant I should be quiet. Then she pulled me aside. "Hush," she said. "Do not ask any more questions. Tomorrow I'll tell you about *Kurd der vourar.*

The next day after lunch, true to her promise, she sat me down and told me this story.

"If a non-Muslim is charged with a crime in Turkey, he is considered guilty until he proves his innocence. If the man charged can't be found because he is in hiding, the police will take his father or brother or cousin. If no male relatives are found then the headmen of his village are taken and tortured until the guilty man surrenders."

Then Grandmom said, "When a Muslim kills a Christian, he believes he has done his God a service. He believes he has made a place for himself in heaven. But when a Christian kills a Muslim, even in self-defense, the Turks take blood revenge. An Armenian will give in to a beating from a Turk he is sure he could easily outfight because he knows he is not alone in his battle. He knows that this family will suffer too. Your father knows that, as a Christian, he would have a hard time in the Turkish courts winning his due over a Muslim. This means that if your papa tries to fight for his house and business against a Turk, he will lose."

I guess I still had a confused look on my face because Grandmom leaned forward on her elbows, blew a puff of smoke from her cigarette in my face, and said, "Now I'll tell you about *kurd der vourar.*

"It is said that a Kurdish Muslim chief in the province of Van once purchased a beautifully engraved sword and was riding proudly with his friends to his village when he came upon an Armenian walking along the road, staff in hand.

"The Kurd said to himself, 'Here is a chance to try out my new sword.' Without hesitating, he slashed at the Armenian's head.

The man held up his staff to protect himself. The Kurd's sword broke. The Kurd caught the Armenian and dragged him before the judge in Agantz and demanded the Armenian pay for the broken sword.

"The poor Armenian begged that he had done nothing but hold his stick over his head to protect himself. He told the judge that the Kurd had broken his own sword.

"The Muslim judge yelled at the Armenian: 'Did you not know that it was a Kurd who was striking you? How dare you put your stick over your head?'

"He made the Armenian pay for the sword, and *Kurd der vourar* — it is a Kurd who strikes — became a fable. So you see, my dear child, it is a hopeless thought for an Armenian to take his claim to a Turkish court. He must always remember *Kurd der vourar.*"

I still did not understand. But Grandmom was finished. "No more questions," she said, dismissing me.

At school, some of my friends talked about recent hangings in town. I wanted to share in their conversations, but I had never seen a hanging. About a week later on my way home from school, about noon, I saw a man walking down the middle of the street with his hands tied behind his back. Turkish soldiers were all around him. They had their guns pushed into his back, as they pushed him down the street. His head was down. I could not see his face. I knew he wasn't a soldier because he was not in uniform. I heard him whispering the Lord's Prayer in Armenian as he passed by me.

More people gathered along the way and followed alongside. I walked in step with the prisoner and tried to see his face. Suddenly, he turned his head to the right in my direction. He looked young, maybe seventeen. I wondered what he had done. Could this be a hanging about to happen? Is this what all the whispers were about? I looked in the crowd for a friend from school. Somehow, I did not want to witness what was about to happen alone.

As we turned the street corner, I saw a large wooden platform in the square ahead. Tall wooden poles were tied in the shape of three triangles, which sat on the wide level landing. A thick rope with a loose knot hanging on the end hung from the center of each triangle.

Around me, people talked in whispers. I sucked in my breath. I was about to witness a hanging and my blood was racing. I looked around for more prisoners. I saw none.

Two guards dragged the young man by his arms. When they got close to the platform, the boy slipped and fell. It took three men to drag him up the steps. They pushed him to the center of the first triangle. Then the tallest soldier on the platform put the loose knot around the boy's neck.

He shouted one word — *Asdvadz eem* — before the trap door under him snapped open. He jerked and kicked his legs in the air. His eyes bulged and his face got red. Then he stopped moving. His eyes were staring wide open when another soldier near the platform sliced open the boy's stomach. His insides hit the ground in a bloody clump and splashed in all directions.

The soldiers cut the rope away from his neck. What was left of his body slowly slid to the ground. The body fell as if in slow motion before my eyes. As his feet touched the earth the rest of his body crumpled in slow folding layers. It seemed to me that his body would never hit the ground and that it would just keep on folding and folding forever. I turned to the wall and vomited.

When I turned back, most of the crowds had gone. There were only a few people left. The body had been taken away but the platform stood like a monster, tall and dark against the hot afternoon sun.

I ran home. "Grandmom, Grandmom, I saw a hanging in the street!"

Grandmom pulled me into the house and shut the door. Vartouhi was close behind. "Tell no one what you saw."

"But I did see."

Grandmom smacked me hard. "You did not see and you did not hear."

Vartouhi started to cry. I was confused.

"Never mention this again," Grandmom said. I ate my dinner that night in silence.

"Why are you so quiet, Ester?" Papa asked.

I looked at Grandmom. Her lips were drawn tight in a mean frown.

"I have a test tomorrow at school," I said, hoping Papa would not ask to see the work. He didn't.

I stopped asking questions. I didn't even talk about the hanging with my friends. It was as though it never happened.

For a while things were quiet in town. There were no more public hangings. But by the end of May, the streets were crowded with soldiers carrying rifles with fixed bayonets on the ends. The Turkish leader of our town gave a speech. He said that all the able-bodied Armenian men who were not in the army already had to present themselves to the soldiers.

"What does able-bodied mean?" I asked Grandmom.

"He means men between fifteen and seventy years of age," she said.

"That means that Papa is able-bodied!"

"No more talk," Grandmom said, leaving the room.

I watched from my window as groups of men gathered daily in the street. Then, bunches of twenty or thirty were marched out of the city by the soldiers. One afternoon, I over-heard some neighbors talking.

One said, "Huh, they won't go very far. As soon as they are outside the city limits they will kill them and come back for more."

During the next few days I watched even more closely as the groups left town. I saw the soldiers march out of town with some men, and a few hours later they returned and took an-other group away. Where did they take them? They came back so soon; did they really kill them? I had so many questions and no answers. We felt lucky because Papa's friends in the government were able to keep him from the daily marches out of town.

But this safety for Papa didn't last long. One night early in June 1915, Papa did not come home from work. We got word the next morning that he had been taken from his butcher shop, along with Katchig and Garabed, to the city jail.

Vartouhi, Grandmom, and I ran to the government building. This building was our city hall, courthouse, and jail all in one. As we entered the large main room, I stretched my neck to see over the bent bodies of men. There, behind bars in a corner of the room, stood Papa. He looked tired. It looked as if he had not slept all night. His clothes were dirty and wrinkled.

"Papa, Papa," I cried. "It's me, Ester, I'm over here." "Hush," Vartouhi said, pinching hard on my arm. "Be quiet. We don't want to catch the eye of the guard."

Papa slid along the walls until he was near the gate and us. I held his hand while he told us how the Turkish soldiers had searched his store. How they had taken all his money and burned his accounting books and stole all the meat in the storehouse.

Then he said, "Don't worry. They told me that I would be released in the morning. They only want to frighten us by keeping us in jail overnight."

"But what about your friend, the Turkish councilman?" I asked.

"I've been told that he is away on business but he will be back next week. I've talked with his assistant and he told me that I will be home tomorrow."

Vartouhi believed him, but Grandmom was sure it was just another Turkish lie.

"No," she said, "let me go to my friend on the council and pay him enough *baksheesh* to get you out tonight."

"It's all right, *Mayrig,* I'll be fine. I believe them. But I haven't had anything to eat and I'm hungry. It would be nice to have some of your hot *abour* tonight. Please bring me some," Papa said.

Grandmom mumbled under her breath something about how Papa was listening and not listening. She wasn't happy, but she agreed to say no more. She promised that she would send me back with a pail of *abour.*

When we got home, Vartouhi hugged Arsen, sat in a corner near the fire, and cried. I could not wait for Grandmom to hand me the pail of soup. I was so excited that I was the one chosen to return to the jail. I felt so important and grown up. I was also happy because I would have another chance to see Papa in the jailhouse. It was exciting to be in the middle of all the people rushing in and out of the official building. Boy, would I have a tale to tell at school tomorrow.

Before I left the house, Grandmom made me wear a *burug.* Only the Turkish women wore this long robe which covered the body from head to toe. The *burug* had narrow eye slits to see through but the slits were so small I saw very little.

"There," she said, "I don't want you to be taken, too. If you wear this *burug* they will think you are Turkish and they will not harm you. Talk to no one. Stop nowhere, and run as quickly as you can to Papa. Then come straight home. Do you understand?"

"Yes, Grandmom."

How did the Turkish women walk without falling, I wondered? I kept tripping over some part of the long flowing thing I was wearing. Finally, I grabbed the coarse material on either side of me and yanked it to my waist and ran. I was careful not to spill the hot *abour* that hung on my arm.

When I arrived back at the jailhouse, the crowds had grown larger. I could not see Papa anywhere. I asked another prisoner to find him and bring him to the side barred window. Everyone in the jail was Armenian. They all knew each another, so it wasn't long before Papa came to the window. I gave him the soup and grabbed his free hand tightly.

"Oh Papa, I'm so scared. What will happen to us without you?" I wept.

"Listen, my child, I'll be home in the morning. I promise that before you go to school, we will have breakfast together just as we always do. The authorities have told me this. They have given me their word. Now hurry home, *atchigess*. It's getting late and dangerous for you to be out on the streets."

I reached up through the bars and hugged his neck very hard. He turned my face to his and kissed me on both cheeks. I never saw Papa again.

Hurrying home, I had to pass by one of the Armenian churches in town. The church was all lit up and there seemed to be a lot of activity, which was unusual because the church was usually dark and quiet during the week. I wondered what the gathering was about, so I ducked behind a wall and watched.

I could hear the voices of the town elders through the windows. The church was full of people and it sounded like some of the people were arguing and yelling at each other.

I heard one man say, "We must fight back. We are like sheep to the slaughter."

Then another voice said, "But we must trust our Turkish friends to their word. If they say we will be safe, I believe them."

"Sure, sure," another said, "You go ahead and believe them and I'll bury your body."

To my left I saw a group of Turkish soldiers on horseback heading toward the church. I crouched down lower behind the wall and watched as a soldier threw a lit torch into an open window.

The other soldiers laughed and shouted, "Let's see your Christian God save you now. You will roast like pigs."

Then the screaming began. The sounds of crying men, women, and children running from the church filled the air. I could not move. I could only listen. The screams got louder as the flames got higher.

I don't know how many escaped or how many did not. I ran home through back streets and fell through the door, coughing and crying.

Grandmom held me tightly to her chest and said, "It's all right, Ester. Calm down, Papa will be here in the morning and he'll know what to do."

I did not tell her what I saw. I told no one what I saw. I could not speak about it. The taste of burning wood was still in my throat. None of us slept that night.

In the morning, a guard from the jail arrived and told us that Papa, along with the other men in the jail, had been sent to a work camp. He told us to pack some things for the short journey. He said it would only be a few days before we met up with Papa. What should we do? It was hard to believe that Papa was gone.

Who was left? Vartouhi was eight months pregnant. Grandmom was old and not very strong. Arsen was just a boy, and me, I was only a young girl with dreams of adventure.

With the memory of the burning church still fresh in my mind, I sat on a corner of the *sadier* with Vartouhi as Grandmom paced the floor. Each of us talked about what we had seen the past few days and tried to put together a plan. We were lost without Papa's wisdom.

Every day large groups of people left town. Then notes came from Papa asking us to leave and meet up with him in the next town. Oh, the thought of seeing Papa again made me happy.

We were told by the local Turkish officials that the enemy was close at hand and that for our own safety, we should leave the city and catch up with our men.

What enemy? Who was close at hand? Those questions were never answered. One of our neighbors, Victor Hamadian, told us that he saw the men of our town taken no further than the outskirts of the city. He said the men were then forced to dig a deep ditch before they were shot and shoved into the human pit.

I faced Mr. Hamadian and said, "How could this be true? Look, we have notes from Papa. He must be alive and only a day's journey away by foot, as his notes say."

Mr. Hamadian was surprised that I would dare question him. A young girl didn't question old men but, suddenly, I was not a young girl anymore. The things I had seen in the past two days gave me the courage to question Mr. Hamadian. I could see Grandmom was uncomfortable. She gave me one of her "be quiet" looks, but I didn't care. I asked Mr. Hamadian again, "How do you know all this?"

Mr. Hamadian leaned over toward me. I thought he was going to yell at me, but instead, he said calmly, "Let me see those notes. I know your father's handwriting and these notes are not from him. Do not believe. Escape now, while you can. If you wait until they tell you to leave, it will be too late."

Again we put our heads together, sat by the fire, and talked through the night.

Grandmom said, "I am too old to walk any distance."

Vartouhi was undecided. She wanted to be with Papa, so she said, "Do you suppose the note is from Papa and our neighbor is wrong?"

The idea of seeing Papa again put her on my side. Arsen had no vote and I chose to go.

I was fifteen, restless, bored with school and my daily routine. I would never become a Muslim and give up my Christianity to stay in Amasia. Some of my schoolmates did this. They married Turkish boys, and, for this, their families' homes and properties were left unharmed. But they had to promise never to speak the Armenian language or practice Christianity again. No, I would not give up my religion. I talked them into leaving. What I didn't know was that it was already too late.

Every day another section of the city was emptied out. My school friend, Aghavni, married a Turk. When I saw her all dressed in satin and silk, gold coins in a band around her forehead, rings and bracelets dripping from her hands, I felt sad. I looked at her face. Her eyes were clouded and her smile was gone.

"Are you happy?" I asked her. She turned her head so I could not see her tears.

"Of course I am," she said. "Only a fool would leave the safety of her home for the unknown. You'll see. You'll be sorry, Ester, and it will be too late."

No, I could not do what she did. I had to leave. During the next three days, we made bread and packed dried apricots, prunes, walnuts, and almonds into ceramic jars. We filled other jars with water and stacked them in our wooden wagon. We stuffed blankets and extra clothes around the jars.

Grandmom sewed into the lining of my tan wool coat many gold pieces and jewelry. The rest of the valuables, gold necklaces, rings, long ropes of woven gold and pearls, she placed in an iron box, which she buried in the soft dirt in a corner of our courtyard. Only Arsen and I knew the hiding place. Grandmom was sure that if anyone would make it back it would be Arsen or me. She was right. All other household goods, furniture, clothing, silver, and rugs were left behind. All we could think about was how things would be better when we met up with Papa.

SEVEN

THE ETERNAL FLAME

MARGARET — JULY 1998

The variegated, angular shapes of the branches on the Japanese bonsai plant caught my eye at the florist's. Standing only six inches high, the tiny tree seemed fluid and mobile, yet it also displayed the formidable strength of a sturdy giant oak. This little plant emitted power by the mere design of its twisted body. It reminded me of Mother, tiny but strong.

Mother was in her room when I arrived. I placed the little plant on her nightstand. She stared at it for a long time before she spoke. Then she laughed.

"You know, I was once twisted like this tree. I bent every which way to make them all happy," she said. "I always gave in and fit in with my surroundings."

"Mother, this plant is shaped by cutting the branches in a certain way so that they can grow in the direction the owner wants them to grow."

"Yes," she said. "That's what they all tried to do to me. They beat me to bend, but I fooled them. I never bent in my heart, only with my body. Margaret, you must not be rigid. A tree that is rigid will break. You must be like this little tree; you must always know when to bend. You know the Turks told me never to speak Armenian. I obeyed. But they couldn't stop me from thinking in Armenian," she said triumphantly, tapping her head with her gnarled finger.

"I remember another time when you wouldn't speak Armenian."

"When was that?" she quickly asked.

"It was November 1979. You called me and announced, 'I'm going to Armenia and you're coming with me.' I told you that I had been to the Soviet Union twice and that that was twice more than anyone should go. You threatened if I didn't go with you, you would go alone."

"I did, didn't I?" she chuckled.

"How could I let you go alone? You were seventy nine years old. You won. We arrived in Yerevan and checked into the Hotel Armenia. Do you remember it?"

"It was a big, old-fashioned building, wasn't it? I remember a fountain across the street from the hotel that spurted pink, blue, and green colored water in the evening," Mother said.

"Do you remember the park around the corner? It was cold that day and you stared at the teenage girls on the swings."

Mother smiled, "One of those girls looked exactly like me when I was a young girl in Amasia."

Then she startled me with, "How about that fat lady that sat outside our room in the hotel. Why was she there?"

81

"She was the watch-lady," I answered.

"Why was she watching us?"

"She was watching everyone, Mother. That's how it was in Russia in 1979. Everyone was under surveillance."

"We didn't do anything. Did we?"

"No, we didn't. But you did refuse to speak Armenian. Why did you do that?" I asked.

Mother smiled, "Tell me what I did."

"When the watch-lady delivered the tea I had ordered, she asked you in Armenian if you wanted lemon or cream. You responded, in your best English, 'I prefer sugar and cream, thank you.' She didn't understand English, so I had to respond for you in Armenian. As a matter of fact, I spoke only Armenian the entire trip and you spoke only English. What was that all about?" I asked.

"Oh, I don't know. I guess I was tired from the trip and English came easier for me."

I reflected for a moment. Perhaps Mother felt frightened. Our roles were reversed, then. She reacted to her surroundings as an American tourist, and I spoke and behaved like an Armenian immigrant returning home.

"The next day our group was taken by bus to the Armenian Martyrs' Monument, do you remember?" I asked Mother.

"Tell me," she said.

"From the distance, the monument's circular structure reminded me of a volcano. Massive slanting columns tilted inward towards each other with no apparent support. As our group walked up the incline to the monument someone handed each of us a red carnation. We entered between the columns. In the center, there was a circular pit with an orange-colored flame. You started crying, remember?"

"Of course I do," Mother said. "Everyone cried. We held hands, and we cried. How could we not cry?

"You moved away from me. Why did you do that?" she asked.

I didn't answer Mother.

I remembered that I needed more space. I needed more air. I drifted to the other side of the flaming circle. Tears wet my cheeks, carrying to my lips the pungent salty brine and mascara.

Behind the monument in the near distance I could see a field of yellow flowers, their heads gently swaying in the breeze as if they, too, were mourning the dead. I tossed my red carnation into the flame and muttered the Lord's Prayer. Mother's and the other women's wailing grew louder as they rocked back and forth.

It was strange. I don't remember feeling sad. What I remember was a warm, comfortable feeling. Then why did I cry? I felt a presence and whispered, "Mother, is that you?" I turned, but there was no one near me. I suddenly felt very cold.

"Hey, wake up, what are you thinking?" Mother was nudging my arm.

"I was wondering whether you were afraid of being captured by the Turks? Is that why you spoke only English in Armenia?" I asked her.

"I guess I was," she said. "It was all such a long time ago. I was a United States citizen but memories of Shamil came back and seemed so fresh. Yes, I guess I was afraid."

"Well, you weren't afraid to speak up to that young college student I hired to take us to the Turkish border so that *we could get a closer look at Mount Ararat and the tomb of St. Gregory the Illuminator. We were almost arrested that day because of your antics."*

Mother giggled. *"He was very handsome. I remember his name, Kevork."*

I was amazed that she remembered his name. Mother remembered so many minor details.

"He told me not to speak English because the border guards might think I was an American spy and shoot me. Hah, border guards! I had escaped many guns in my life. He was no threat. You left me alone and went down into that tomb with him. I always wondered what went on down there," she queried slyly.

"When Kevork and I climbed down the wall ladder into the pit where St. Gregory had been imprisoned, I was really worried about leaving you behind. You remember Kevork made me leave my purse with you because it would be too difficult to climb down and hold onto it at the same time. That really made me nervous. All our money, tickets, and passports were in my purse."

"You did act a little crazy about that purse. Go on. Go on. Tell me what happened in the pit."

"Well, there was no light, and it was hard descending. There was almost no space between the walls and the iron bars that had been hammered into the rock as steps. I remember Kevork went first. His hand guided my feet to each metal strip. At the bottom we stood in the dark a long time while Kevork searched his pockets for a match to light the two candles he was clever enough to bring with him. He regaled me with facts about St. Gregory the Illuminator. It seems that St. Gregory had been thrown into this pit in 301 A.D. by the Zoroastrian King Tiridates for proselytizing. He survived to cure the king,

because the king's mother, a convert, secretly threw food to him every night.

"When I looked up and saw just a tiny patch of sky through the pit opening, all reverence for St. Gregory left me. I really feared that this would be my final resting place. Kevork found his matches. We lit our candles and mumbled a quick prayer to Gregory. I convinced him that leaving you alone, speaking only English, with the border guards, was not a good idea. Fear of being trapped in that hole energized me so much I practically flew up the walls."

"So that's why you returned so quickly. I was enjoying the view of Mount Ararat."

"Do you believe that Noah really landed his ark on Mount Ararat?" I asked Mother.

"How should I know? I wasn't there. That was before my time."

I closed my eyes and the image of Mount Ararat appeared to me as clearly as it did that day in 1979. The stark white frozen blanket of snow near the summit was capped by floating clouds resting now and then like huge marshmallows around its perimeter. The sky was cobalt blue. Streaks of yellow and magenta splashed in and out of the deep crevasses like the colors in a Van Gogh painting.

I had looked west that day, thinking Amasia was on the other side of those mountains. The road Mother and her family had marched over was in that direction. I remember turning my face into the setting sun. The waning rays burned. I closed my eyes.

I thought about the day Mother and her family left their beloved Amasia. I thought about the long road she had traveled, to me and my father; to my children, her grandchildren; to this home, here, in New York. A whole life. And then I saw myself, Margaret, on the road with her, years and years ago, before I was even born, just a speck traveling lightly in the air beside her; I had always been hers. I had always been here, with her. Her history was mine. Her death, when it happened, could mean only one thing. I was next in line.

Let this story live larger than we ever could.

EIGHT

THE KNOCK AT THE DOOR

ESTER — JUNE 1915

The morning before we planned to leave, *zaptiyehs* came pounding on our door. A youthful Turkish soldier with the authority, might, and terror of the Turkish army in his voice, shouted that we had to leave immediately.

"Whoever remains will be shot," he said. "Move along, *yallah, yallah*."

Two other soldiers were standing behind him with large rifles in their hands. I backed up against the far wall. Vartouhi threw her shoulders back and stood tall.

"How can we leave so quickly?" she said, catching her breath between words. "We need to prepare."

"That's not my business," the soldier said. "Just gather some things and leave."

The three *zaptiyehs* looked no older than I did. Fuzzy hairs of manhood were just starting to pop out on their faces. They were just boys carrying guns almost as big as they were. The boy's thin hand wrapped around the shining wood handle of the gun. With his other hand he rubbed the dull gray metal of the barrel up and down. It was a crazy thought, but at that moment I couldn't help but wonder how often he polished the handle to make it shine so much.

I took a closer look at their faces. Why, they looked like my classmates from school. Could they shoot me? Would they shoot me? I tried to understand why this terrible thing was happening; but all I could think was, we had waited too long. We should have left before they came for us. We should have listened to Haroutoun.

Aksor — the deportation word everyone in town was whispering. What did it mean? What would it be like? There was no time to think. With Papa gone, we were on our own.

Vartouhi quickly tied a canvas over our open wagon filled with food and blankets. She hitched a single cow to pull it, and we fled, joining the caravan of wagons leaving Amasia. In my haste, I left my tan wool coat hanging behind the door. I never thought I'd see that coat again.

We were only a half hour out of town when a group of Kurds charged down from the mountains and attacked the first group at the front of the caravan. Then the *zaptiyehs* started grumbling. Someone in the group said they were there to protect us from the Kurds. This was a lie, because these soldiers attacked us along with the Kurds. Swinging their curved swords in the air over their heads, screaming and shouting curses, they rode their horses straight into the slow-moving crowd of people.

I slipped to the ground. Around me people were screaming. Some were crushed under wagon wheels; others were bleeding from various parts of their bodies. One horse stomped on a woman next to me and I heard the loud cracking of her bones breaking. It was like the sound of Grandmom cracking walnuts, only louder. Another man near me was stuck under a broken wagon wheel. He was holding onto a woman's hand. Her head was missing! Those who were not killed on the first charge were robbed and beaten.

Then the soldiers came for the girls. The prettiest ones were taken first. I watched as soldiers lifted some of the girls by their hair and threw them over the backs of their horses. Then they rode away.

"Asdvadz eem!" cried Grandmom. She pushed me down in the wagon and scratched my face with a sharp rock and rubbed raw garlic and mud into the creases. Grandmom always carried garlic in her pocket to keep away the evil eye.

Then, with a satisfied tone in her voice, she said, "There, this will fester and weep and you will look ugly. Quickly, put on these baggy clothes, and maybe the soldiers won't want you. Keep your head down and be still."

After the attack, it was very quiet. We moved slowly with the rest of the group. Around us the silence hung heavy like thick fog. By morning, my face was itching and oozing with white pus. I grabbed Vartouhi's small hand mirror. Who was this creature staring back at me? I turned away with disgust at the sight of my face, the same face that many had said was a pretty face. I looked like a monster. No one looked at me. Grandmom was pleased with her handiwork.

Our group slowly moved ahead. Grandmom and Vartouhi rode in the wagon. Arsen and I walked close by. By nightfall, the caravan stopped. Amasia was behind us. I fell into a deep sleep. Through the night, I heard the cries of babies and women screaming in the darkness. I turned my head to a bright, blazing light in the sky. Could it be sunrise already? I turned to Grandmom and whispered, "Is it morning?"

"No, Ester, it's not the rising sun, it is houses in Amasia burning." Smoke and flying embers filled the air like fireflies on a summer night. I crouched down low and prayed. Was this the good luck I was waiting for each year when I found the coin in my *choreg* at Christmas? Finding that coin was supposed to guarantee me a year of good luck and happy times. Not this.

That morning, after we had been walking for three hours, the soldiers attacked the slow-marching caravan again. This time our supplies and wagon were taken. We walked on the inside of the mass of bodies because the people on the outer edges were whipped and trampled by the soldiers on horseback. Grandmom kept pushing me into the center if I strayed a little. Arsen held my hand tightly and Vartouhi struggled to keep up. We walked this way for three days and three nights. All we had to eat was some *cheoreg* that Grandmom had in her pocket. She broke it into three pieces, one for Vartouhi, Arsen, and me. She had none.

There were about a hundred in our group. Ahead of us was another group a little larger, and behind us a third group about the same size. Some whispered that our destination was the death camp in the desert of Der-el-Zor. It was rumored that those who made it to the death camp were the strong ones, most died along the way. For the first time, I wondered if we would make it to Der-el-Zor or be among those who died.

It was a hot June, and what little water we had was drying

up because of the heat. I held on to a small water jug I had saved from our wagon, but it was almost empty. The next night we camped near a well. The Turkish soldiers filled their canteens and water jars to the brim.

After they finished, they shouted to the crowd, "Anyone caught trying to get water will be shot."

We sat close to each other, our bodies touching. No one went near the well. Later that same night we heard a woman's scream coming from the direction of the well. Nobody moved. In the morning we saw the body of a young bride we knew from Amasia. A water jug was hanging from her blackish-blue fingers. Someone said she had been stabbed many times. I saw her pregnant stomach sliced open and her unborn baby stuck on a sword that was shoved in the dirt near her head. As we walked past, Vartouhi pushed my face into her chest so I could not see, but I had already seen it all very clearly.

The middle of the next day we passed a deep pit by the side of the road filled with the naked bodies of young and old men. I leaned over as far as I could to see if Papa was one of the dead. There were so many crumbled shapes, heads under feet, hands frozen stiff toward the sky, mouths open, and eyes unblinking. There was no real sound, but I could feel pressure in my ears as though I were hearing voices. I must be crazy, I thought. How can one hear silence?

"Move, move along," the *zaptiyehs* shouted.

Arsen hung on my arm and cried. I could hear Grandmom saying the Lord's Prayer over and over. Vartouhi held her pregnant stomach with both hands as she marched. We hadn't eaten for five days when we came upon some women so thin that the skin hung on their bones. I wondered how many days would pass before we looked the same. A tiny baby was sucking on the breast of its dead mother, while other women were tearing pieces of flesh from the bodies left by the road. Arsen yanked hard on my arm.

"Please, please, promise me you will not let anyone eat my body except you."

"Arsen, don't talk crazy. No one is going to eat your body."

"No, no, you must promise me now," he said.

I was weary. "All right, I promise."

We had stopped for rest by the side of the road when Kamal Bey, the leader of our group of *zaptiyehs,* shouted to his men. "Attack, attack!"

Someone said he was angry because he had picked a beautiful Armenian girl for himself, but rather than go to him, she cut her wrists. Wagons were overturned. The sound of bullets filled the air. People near me were stabbed. Some tried to run away, but they were run over by the soldiers' horses. They circled us as if we were a herd of cattle.

There was no escape. We lay very still for a long time not talking, not moving. Around us lay the dead and near-dead. After their assault, the soldiers backed off to the edge of the group. Slowly, we rose, gathered together our few belongings, and marched again. We had one quilt, one enamel cup, and some dried apricots and almonds that Grandmom had picked off a corpse. Well, I think it was a corpse. Grandmom passed a body lying beside the road. She pushed what appeared to be a man's body with her cane. There was no movement. Thinking the man was dead, she went through his pockets and found the stale apricots and almonds. It was the first solid food I'd had in five days. We had no water. I tied the quilt to my shoulders and carried Arsen. Vartouhi and Grandmom walked slowly close by.

I felt the weight of hands on my back. A dirty old man with

a beard down to his chest grabbed my shoulders and said, "Come with me, foolish girl. You have no chance. You will be killed. I can save you."

"No!" I screamed. "Get away from me." I pushed myself into the crowd dragging Arsen by the arm. The old man followed another young girl. I never saw either of them again.

The ground was dry and cracked. The following day shortly after sunrise dark clouds swept across us, turning day into night. High winds gathered up the loose dirt under our feet and whipped sand and leaves into our faces. I covered my face with my hands, but the thin sand found its way into my eyes and mouth. It was hot and wet. I could not breathe. My nose was filled with this sticky muddy sand. Lightning flashed and hit the ground nearby. When it struck again I was sure that some people near me were hit because the screaming got very loud at the very same moment.

Then the rain came. The weight of the water pushed me to the ground. Some people nearby tried to fit under our quilt. There must have been fifteen or more bodies covered by that quilt. A hand, a head, half a body, a finger. Everyone was looking for some cover from the pounding rain.

Then a flood of water rushed down from a hill close by, bringing with it a mixture of small rocks, sand, mud, and all kinds of human filth. The little children were the saddest. Some slipped right out of their mothers' arms and disappeared into the thick mud. The lightning, thunder, and pounding rain seemed to make the soldiers crazy. They attacked us harder than before, as we ran to get away from them. I tried to fill my small cup with some of the water that spilled from the corner of the quilt. I collected only drops.

We held on to each other, afraid to move. I looked for Arsen. He was gone.

"Arsen, Arsen, where are you?" I called. It was quiet. Then I heard some whimpering to my left.

"Arsen is that you?" No, it wasn't. Sometime during the night, he had been taken. I never felt his tiny hand leave mine.

"It's my fault. I should have held on to him tighter," I said to Grandmom. But she didn't hear me. She and Vartouhi were crying and praying for God to save us.

Now we were three.

Every so often, the leader of the Turkish soldiers would bend down from his horse, take hold of a small child by the arm and twist the body in the air. Then he'd smash the baby to the ground.

He shouted loudly to all listening, "Don't think that I have killed an innocent child. Even these newborn babies are criminals, because they carry the seeds of vengeance. Kill the children, too."

I heard the soldiers say, "Kill the children too. Kill them all." I put my hands over my ears but I could still hear them.

Ahead in the distance, I saw smoke rising from the lower side of the mountain.

"Grandmom, look it's a town! We'll be saved," I said.

Grandmom lifted her eyes toward the sky and slowly moved her head from side to side. "It's only the group ahead of us, my child. The smoke you see is the steam caused by the hot sun on the wet tents. Just steam, my child, just steam."

I watched some women a few feet away eating the flesh of a dead horse. Though I hadn't eaten for days, I felt no hunger. I wondered, "Is Arsen dead? Is someone eating his flesh?"

There was no time for anyone to mourn the dead. Those who were alive marched along, hoping to escape the next attack. Grandmom was walking more and more slowly. The soldiers cracked their whips across our backs to make us move faster. Grandmom fell. I grabbed her. I carried her on my back for a while before she fell again.

"Go on without me," she whispered. "I'm old, I will not make it, but you must live."

Then she reached up and pulled a little blackened iron cross from her neck. She stuffed it into my hand and said, "Keep this, Ester, and pray for God's help."

I reached for her again, but a soldier on horseback came between us. I was pushed ahead with the others. She was left behind. I turned to look for Grandmom and saw the butt of a rifle coming down on her head. A splash of red flew through the air.

I shouted, "Grandmom, Grandmom!" but I knew she would never hear me again. What kind of God could let this happen? The little cross was burning in my hand. Women ran screaming in all directions during the killing. They rushed ahead to get away from the dead.

Now we were two.

I looked at Vartouhi. Her hair had turned gray. When did this happen? Could one's hair turn gray in days? Would mine turn gray too? Her dress was torn and her arms were scratched and bleeding. Would she die? Would I be alone? Vartouhi was all I had left. She could not die. I thought of the poor people getting ready to leave their hometowns as we had. If only they could be warned. But they probably wouldn't believe, just as we hadn't.

The next night Vartouhi had her baby. I rubbed her stomach as she twisted and turned in pain. I had never seen a baby born. Only midwives and older women understood such things. I was always pushed out of the room. I saw some women I did not know holding Vartouhi down by her shoulders.

"Keep her down or the soldiers will see us," said one. Hiding behind a tree, with strange hands covering her mouth to cut off her screams, Vartouhi gave birth. It happened so fast I was surprised when the spot I was rubbing on her belly suddenly went flat and a baby slowly came out from under her on the soft dirt.

"It's a boy, Ester, it's a boy," Vartouhi said.

Quickly, two more women came to help. They buried the slimy afterbirth with more care than they did the dead we left along side of the road. The burying of the afterbirth was a custom the women would not give up, even on this death march. Barely able to stand from the pain of her labor, Vartouhi picked up her newborn baby and marched with the rest of us for six hours. We gathered some weeds and dandelions and boiled up a broth for Vartouhi in a small pot of water that one of the women shared. The baby cried all the time. Vartouhi's dried up breasts had no milk.

Still hopeful, I said, "Perhaps when we catch up with Papa, he will have food and water for us." Vartouhi looked at me sadly.

The next day another old, partially crippled man pushed through the crowd and pulled Vartouhi to her knees by the side of the road. He pointed to me as he whispered in her ear. A few minutes later, Vartouhi crawled over to me and said, "He will take care of us if you will be his. Please, go with him. I'll be your servant."

"No, no, I can't. You go with him and I'll be your servant." She didn't seem to understand what I was saying. Again she started to beg me. Out of the corner of my eye, I saw the old man coming towards me. I turned and ran. The ground fell away under my feet and I slid down a steep hill. I rolled over rocks and broken glass. They cut through my knees and hands as I slid along the surface. I lay at the bottom, my knees badly cut and bleeding. I could not stand. Someone I did not see carried me back up the hill and lifted me onto a donkey.

"Sure, she wants to save herself by sacrificing this poor child. Why should she care. She's only her stepmother," a woman a few feet away whispered.

That woman was wrong. Vartouhi gave her last few coins to the donkey owner so that I could ride. She carried her baby and walked alongside.

I rode for several hours. The pain in my legs crept up my back. My head was hot and sweaty. I fell.

Someone shouted, "Look, look, she has fallen off the donkey." A few heads turned. Tired faces stared blankly then shuffled on. No one had the strength or will to help. Vartouhi put her baby down on a rock and lifted me back on the donkey. My face felt like it was on fire and my breath came in short gasps.

"She's burning with fever," a voice said.

My legs were swollen and covered with yellow, crusty scum.

When I fell again, a soldier pushed Vartouhi away. "Leave her, she'll be dead soon anyway."

I lay by the side of the road near a campsite where a tribe of Kurds waited for the passing caravans. I watched as they robbed the dead and the almost-dead. An old woman crept close and whispered in Turkish that she was Armenian.

"They do not know I'm Armenian," she said. "You must not say a word." She told me she cooked for the Kurds and kept their tents in order. She said her name was Seranoush but the Kurds gave her a Turkish name. They called her Kardesoglu.

Vartouhi slipped back from the crowd and found me with this woman.

She begged, "Please, when this child is dead remove the handkerchief pinned to her underskirt. In it, you will find a gold ring and chain. Take them from her and when you return to Amasia, bring them with you as proof of her death."

I heard the woman say, "I have seen many with typhus. This one has it, she won't live long."

Vartouhi leaned down and kissed my forehead. She looked up to the sky and whispered, *"Asdvadz, atchigees azadey."* (God save my little girl.) I watched her disappear into the crowd of marching refugees.

I was alone. My body was covered with lice and weeping sores. Seranoush dragged me down to the edge of the nearby river.

"Here, take this cup, and pour the cool water over your body. It may break your fever." Before she left me, she said, "I'll bring you some *tahn* and bread when it's safe."

All day long in the blazing sun, I poured water over my body to lower my fever and wash off some of the pus and lice. I watched many bodies float past me in the river. There were arms, legs, and parts of broken bodies. Some got caught in the brush floating by. I prayed for God to take me too.

I rested my head against the spoke of a broken wagon wheel. At night, Seranoush dragged me closer to the tent site but never inside. She was afraid if the Kurds saw me they would kill me. She fed me some scraps of food left over from their plates. But mostly I lived on yogurt mixed with water and bread for the next six days.

At night, under the thin blanket Seranoush had given me, I stared up at the dark blue sky filled with thousands of white dots. How clear and bright the stars were against the darkness! The moon flooded soft light through a clump of bushes. I remembered my happy days at our *aikee*. This same moon looked down on me then and now. I could not help but wonder if the moon could think and, if so, what was it thinking now. So little time had passed, but my world had been turned upside down. Was this really happening? Would I wake to see Papa reaching out for my hand for our walk to school?

Seranoush followed the same pattern every day. She brought me extra yogurt to rub on my sores, along with the *tahn* and dry bread I ate to keep me alive. The pain was so bad I kept praying for God to take me.

One morning, Seranoush leaned over and whispered in my ear. *"Seni öldüreyim mi?"* The Turkish words, "Shall I kill you?"

"Why do you ask this crazy question? Yes! Yes, do it quickly," I answered.

"No, my child, God will take you when it is your time. It is not for me to do."

What a stupid woman, I thought. Why did she ask the question if she wasn't going to do it?

I was in a deep sleep one morning when some Kurds came along and thought I was dead. They took off my clothes and tossed me into a wagon filled with naked dead bodies. I lay there, not moving under the pile of rotting flesh. I opened my eyes slightly and stared right into an open skull. Even through the mass of blood, I could see the sections of the brain. It was neat and orderly. I was not surprised to see blue and green in the mess because I had seen pictures of a skull that looked just like this when I was in school. The almost disconnected head seemed to belong to a young boy about Arsen's age. His eyes were open and his mouth was grinning. Did I know him? Could he be alive with his head split open? Suddenly, another body was tossed over me, and I slipped deeper into the pit of slimy flesh. I didn't move. I was afraid if they discovered I wasn't dead, they would kill me. But wasn't that what I wanted? I was silent. I held my head still in a small pocket of foul air.

The horses backed up to the edge of a steep drop-off, and the back wall of the wagon was opened. I rolled out with the rest of the bodies and slid over the edge of a cliff. A tree limb sticking out of a rock stopped me from falling into the river below.

"Look, one is stuck on that tree," said the wagon-driver.

"Don't worry: the wind will push the bitch soon enough. I'm hungry, let's go," said his helper.

I lay still. In the near distance I saw the large black rounded arches of Kirgoz bridge. The wagon moved on. I learned later that as the wagon drivers passed the campsite, Seranoush asked about a girl with my description.

"Oh yes, she was dead," the wagon driver answered, "so we dumped her upriver with the last load of bodies."

When it was safe, Seranoush searched and found me hanging on the branch over the ledge. Surprised I was not dead, she pulled me up.

I don't know why she came for me and saved my life again. She never told me.

"Let me die. Push me over the edge. What have I left? Why should I live? You asked to kill me. Now I say, let me go. Let the river be my grave."

Seranoush leaned over and whispered in my ear, *"Boud-a-getchere."*

I could hardly hear her.

"What? What?"

Again she whispered, "Ester, *Bou da getchere*. This, too, will pass."

I closed my eyes. It was three weeks since we had left Amasia; it felt like three years.

NINE

THE EVIL EYE

MARGARET — AUGUST 1998

It was a balmy August day when my daughter, Lynn, and grandchildren, Raymond and Sara, and I drove to New York from Pennsylvania to visit Mother. When Mother saw us, she giggled and clapped her hands. The children clapped too.

"Mother, be careful you don't prick your finger on this cactus," I said as I handed her the prickly vertical plant.

"Hmmm, let me see it up close," Mother said. "I saw plants like this growing along the side of the road when we left Amasia."

"They require little water to survive," I said. "That's probably why they were growing wild."

"We needed water to march, but the soldiers would not let us have any. When Seranoush saved me from the death march and got me to Yousouf Bey's house, I thought my troubles were over."

Mother leaned back holding the cactus firmly in her hand.

"Yousouf Bey promised to take care of me like a daughter."

Staring at the phallic shaped cactus, Mother murmured softly, "But he raped me."

"What, what did you say?" I leaned forward, wondering if the children had heard what she said.

"Sometimes old memories creep into my head, but I just push them away. It's better that way," Mother said softly.

I was relieved that she did not continue her story about Yousouf Bey.

"Can we play out in the garden, Great Grandmom?" Sara asked cheerfully.

"Sure, why not?" Mother answered. "I could use some fresh air."

Mother watched intently as Raymond and Sara climbed trees and scurried in and out of a wooden gazebo strategically situated in the center of the vast lawn. A gentle breeze blew a few short hairs into her eyes. I brushed them back. Mother grabbed my hand, pressed it to her forehead, then kissed it.

"You know, we had something like that at our aikee*," she said, pointing to the gazebo. "I watched the workers of our* aikee *build the house. First they laid wooden boards flat, side by side. The walls went up and in a day the house was built. Colorful rugs were laid on the floor as covering. Men from neighboring* aikees *came by nightly to visit and talk about many things with Papa. They sat cross-legged in a circle and smoked hand-rolled cigarettes while the women served food*

and drinks. They talked about their crops, the weather, and local politics. My Papa liked going to our aikee because it was a chance for him to relax away from the city noises."

Lynn showed mother a photo from last Christmas.

"Oh, there I am. I was heavier then," Mother said. She turned to me, "Don't get fat, it's not healthy. Eat everything in moderation, and watch what you drink, wine makes you fat. Sometimes I think you drink too much wine."

Sometimes I do, Mother, sometimes I do. I mentally noted that I should be more moderate in my eating and drinking habits.

This was not the first time Mother had chastised me for overindulging.

"Do you still have that pillow your mother needle pointed for you?" Mother asked Lynn.

"Sure, Grandmom, look at the picture again. There it is, next to you on the sofa."

"Bou da getchere, 'this, too, shall pass,' remember that always," Mother said to Lynn. "No matter what happens to you in life, remember those words. Saying bou da getchere again and again kept me alive many times. When I was close to death and alone on the road, a woman named Seranoush whispered it in my ear and saved my life."

Lynn smiled, "I'll remember, Grandmom, and when I say those words I'll think of you. Here, I brought you some cherries. Do you like cherries?"

"Cherries! I ate more cherries than anyone at our aikee," Mother chirped. "When my family and I went to our farm for the summer, I'd climb all the trees, just like Sara and Raymond. We had lots of cherry trees and many workers to pick the fruit. While the workers filled basket after basket, I'd sit in the tree and eat cherries.

"One day, my Papa shouted to me as I sat on a branch, 'Ester, where is your basket?' I tapped my stomach and said, 'Here's my basket, and it's almost full.'"

Sara and Raymond giggled. "That's the best kind of basket, Great Grandmom. I think I'll try that when we pick strawberries," Sara said, turning toward Lynn.

"Oh, no you won't," Lynn scolded. "You'll surely get a bad tummy ache."

Lynn turned to Mother, "You know, Grandmom, Sara's riding is improving and soon she will compete in Arabian horse shows."

Mother tilted her head back. "I had a horse when I was Sara's age. His name was Aragats. I don't know what kind of horse he was, but he was fifteen hands high and white as snow. He ran like the wind."

I said nothing; I was too busy remembering something I had read in Michael Arlen's Passage to Ararat. *During the time of Xerxes (520 BCE–465 BCE), as many as 25,000 horses were sent down from Armenia to Persia every year. The high altitude of the Armenian plateau combined with the terrain produced a short, thick, dry grass, very rich in protein. This made it an unusually fine place to breed strong horses capable of running long distances at top speed.*

Is it possible that my daughter and granddaughter have inherited their love of Arabian horses from their ancient Armenian ancestors?

My thoughts were interrupted by the voices of two women residents strolling by us in the garden.

"So, Ester, I see you are enjoying your family," one said.

"Vailey!" the other said.

Mother slyly smiled as they moved past us.

"Quick!" Mother said. "Mod et treh. Wrap your fore-

finger over your thumb and point it at those ladies. Mod et treh," she sternly ordered.

I followed her direction.

"But Mother, they were just being friendly."

"No," Mother said, "The evil eye comes from the jealous compliments of others. I know they are envious because their children never visit. It is lonely here without visitors. Good, you put your finger to them. You are safe now from their evil eye."

Sara thoughtfully watched and listened. She was six. She didn't understand. But I did.

Raymond whispered in my ear.

"I'm bored, Grammy."

Two hours had passed. I realized how difficult it must be for a seven year old to be surrounded by aged people shuffling about. Strange skeletal hands reached out to pat him on the head and pinch his cheek as they passed, each needing to touch the spark of youth, hoping perhaps to capture some of the electricity emanating from his energetic young body. Raymond jumped away from these touches and moved closer to Great Grandmom. He leaned over and hugged her. She smiled and hugged him back.

"Raymond," I said, "remember this day, because sometime in the future your son will say, 'I'm bored, Dad.' That will be the day you are visiting me in a home like this one."

One of the passing women abruptly turned around and announced, "I'm Mairam, I'm just a visitor here. My daughter went on vacation so I'm here while she is away."

Wow, I thought, an overnight sitting service for senior citizens!

"I heard you asking your mother about the 'dark time' in Turkey. I lived through the genocide just like your mother. I was only four when the Turks massacred the people in my *town. And do you know what? The Turks say it never happened."*

Mother chimed in with, "The Turks were jealous of us. We had the best farmlands and the best businesses. But why did they have to kill us?"

All I could muster was, "I don't know; it was a terrible time, Mother."

Both elderly women mumbled in unison. "Why did they do it? Why do they still say it never happened?"

I had no answers. I hugged Mother and kissed her brow.

"You're my baby," she murmured. "How you've grown. You were like Raymond and Sara not so long ago. Where did the years go?"

Again, I had no answers. I held her hands in mine. I ran my fingers down her back. Her vertebrae felt strangely spiky and fragile. I wanted to stay longer.

Each time I left Mother, I'd think, is this the last time I'll see her alive?

I had to get out before anyone saw my tears. I raised my voice and cheerfully said, "Come on, I'll take you in before we leave." Then, hurriedly, "I'll call you later, Mother."

I got in the car and turned my face toward the window. I didn't want the children to see me crying. A little hand crept over mine. I turned my head. Sara, just six years old, was cradling my hand in hers. She had watched me stroking Mother's hand and now she was caressing mine the same way. Slowly, gingerly, she fondled my palm. Neither of us spoke.

Overhead, I heard the sound of a crow cawing and the roar of an airplane landing at nearby LaGuardia Airport. Then it was quiet. I listened into the silence. I imagined my mother, lying nearly dead, begging for death by the side of that river.

Sometimes I feel terror so acute, so delineated, the world closes in. Terror, like genes, gets passed down, from him to her, from you to me.

I looked at Sara. What would she inherit? She was still holding my hand. I pulled away. I did it, understand, out of love. I did it to keep her safe.

TEN

BOU DA GETCHERE

The hot July sun bore down on me as I lay beside the river bank. Two weeks had passed since Seranoush had dragged me off the cliff. Every day she bathed my body with yogurt to lower my fever. Soon the fever went down and my swollen legs returned to their normal shape. Although I walked with a cane, I could feel myself getting stronger every day.

One morning as I washed my face in the river I slid my hands over my arms and legs. I could feel my veins under the surface of my skin. My skin had always been taut, healthy and bursting with the flow of blood. But now my skin didn't feel as though it was part of my body. I was not the same girl I once was. Who was I?

Days passed. With my fever gone, my hair combed and clean clothes, I looked a little more human. I helped Seranoush carry water and prepare food for the Kurds in the camp and the Turkish soldiers passing through. When serving and picking up after the men, I was careful to keep my eyes directly on the floor. If I looked a Kurd in the eye he might think I was inviting him to touch me. I didn't need any more trouble than I already had.

Several weeks later, Seranoush told me about a Turkish man and his wife who lived just down the road near Malatya.

"It's not far from here, Ester. Yousouf Bey and his wife need a housekeeper," she said, "I'll recommend you because they want a girl from a good family with proper breeding. Will you go?"

Malatya was the direction that Vartouhi and the caravan had gone. Perhaps I could catch up with her. I wanted to believe she was still alive and still walking.

"Yes, if they'll have me, I'll work for them."

Seranoush helped me crawl into the back of an empty wagon while the driver ate his dinner in the tent. She had paid him with free food and some coins to deliver us to Malatya. She shoved the coin and ring that Vartouhi had given her back into my hand and said, "Take these. Now that you are well you can have them back. I won't have to show them to prove your death."

"Seranoush, you risked your life to save mine. I want you to keep them."

"But you have no money. You may need these, Ester."

I pressed them back into her hand. I knew it was the right thing to do. I looked at Seranoush, searching her eyes for advice. "What will I do if they don't want to keep me?" I asked.

"Don't worry; they'll keep you. Just say little and remember never speak even one word of Armenian. If you do, you'll be sent back to the caravan. Don't worry, you'll be fine. Pray to God."

The journey was a short distance by wagon. Seranoush introduced me to Yousouf Bey and his wife, Hanum, at their front door. She gave me one final hug then turned and headed back to the wagon for the return trip to the campsite.

It was late when I arrived, so Hanum quickly took me to the second floor and said, "This will be your room. We'll talk in the morning."

I was so tired I fell into bed and slept soundly. Early the next morning, Hanum woke me.

"Come now, I'll show you the rest of the house."

The house was big, with many large rooms filled with antique furniture and paintings, the kind I had seen of English and French homes in my schoolbooks. Silver, crystal, and silk rugs seemed to be everywhere.

Yousouf Bey was old. He pushed his runny nose close to my face and mumbled, "Can you cook?"

Before I could answer, Hanum said, "Ester will help me with other household chores. There is no need for her to cook."

Hanum was short and very thin. She wore her straight, gray hair parted down the middle. Her face was wrinkled and she looked tired, the way that Vartouhi looked after a day of washing clothes and beating rugs.

Hanum pressed me against her chest and said, "Don't worry. You are safe from the killing here. I never had any children; you will be the daughter I've always wanted, Ester."

She smelled like our lilac bush in Amasia. Her long hair fell over my shoulder. Could this woman be as nice as she seemed?

Hanum smiled. I wanted to believe her kindness was real, but Haroutoun's words rang in my ears, "Remember, trust no one."

Also in the house, working as house boys, were Aram and Souren from Amasia. I didn't know them but I had seen them from a distance at church functions. Hanum introduced us before they went about their daily tasks.

"Ester, there are some shirts and skirts for you in the closet in your room. See if they fit you," Hanum said.

I changed into a clean shirt and looked around the room where I had slept last night. How different it was in the light of day. It was as though I had entered a garden. Brightly colored floral paintings hung on the wall. Rose-colored silk curtains draped over the windows and slippery satin sheets trimmed with lace covered the bed. Colorful floral rugs spilled across the floor like a field of wild flowers. I felt safe.

I helped the cook wash and prepare vegetables. I served the meals and helped Hanum with the gardening, ironing and sewing. I had little contact with the boys, as their chores were mostly outside. Several weeks passed. It was late August, 1915.

One morning, from the open window in my room, I overheard Aram and Souren talking in Armenian near the house.

Aram said, "When I grow up, I'm coming back here to kill all the Turks."

I peered out the window. Souren's eyes got big as he listened to his friend describe in detail, in Armenian, how he was going to do this. Hanum came into the room just then and heard them too.

I turned away from the window. She gave me a look and said, "What are they talking about?"

I caught my breath, looked straight into her eyes, and said, "Oh, Aram told Souren that one day he would teach him how to swim in your great pond."

"That's nice," Hanum said. Then she leaned out the window and called to the boys in Turkish, "Go ahead, teach him how to swim now while it is still warm enough."

The boys looked up, confused.

Later, I told them to be more careful where they talked. "What if someone besides me had heard you? Do not speak Armenian. You know it's not allowed and you will be beaten if you are caught. You were lucky that it was Hanum and not Yousouf Bey who heard you."

Aram threw his shoulders back and said, "When I learn to speak Turkish well enough to pass as a Turk, I'll escape over the border to Russia and sign up with the Armenian revolutionary forces."

I grabbed Aram's shirt collar and pulled his head close to my lips. "Listen to me, the Turk is not as stupid as you think. Let me tell you a story I heard about another young boy just your age that said the same thing. A Turkish officer stopped him at the border, suspecting that he was not Turkish. He pulled down his pants and saw that he was not circumcised. He pulled out his knife and stuck it into the boy's heart."

Their eyes grew big and their mouths were shut tight.

"See," I said, "speaking Turkish will not stop them from finding out you are an Armenian. Now be quiet or we'll all be killed because of your stupid talk."

Every night for the next several weeks I had nightmares and night sweats. Soon I gained enough strength to walk without using a cane. One evening, Yousouf Bey, who was a retired officer in the Turkish Army, had some military guests for dinner. Hanum put a long dark brown *burug* on me and reminded me not to speak in the presence of the men.

I remembered the last time I wore a *burug*. I was at the jailhouse in Amasia visiting my father for the last time. That same night the Turks burned our church. That same night I watched and listened to the screams of those trying to escape. That same night no help came.

Catching me daydreaming, Hanum squeezed my hand and said, "Come, Ester, help me serve the coffee."

As I passed around the coffee and honey cakes, the men around the table started to boast and tell stories. One told the story of a young couple he had captured in one of the convoys.

"They were about fifteen years old," he said. "The boy had very little hair on his face. He was also very thin and short. The girl was taller than the boy. She wore her hair in a single thick braid down her back. Both wore long woolen dresses to cover their bodies. They thought they could fool us by pretending they were sisters.

"'Oh, please do not separate me from my sister. She is sick and needs my help,' one said.

"'All right, *Janum*, I'll take you both,' I said. After I raped the one, I reached for the other and realized I had a boy instead. So I cut off his genitals with my sword. 'There, now you are a girl, how do you like it?' Then my men and I propped the boy up against a wall so he could watch us take turns sodomizing the girl. Afterward, we tied the two together and threw them into the river, where they floated for a short while before the tide carried them away. They never made a sound."

Laughter and applause filled the air.

"What a good way to take care of those two Armenians," one man said.

Then a fat man at the end of the table spoke, "Well, I have an even better story to tell. After a long day of beating and killing many, my brothers and I came upon a new group of Armenians. We were tired, but more had to be killed. So we bent the Armenians over a dry well and with one swoop of our swords we could cut off four heads at one time. Doing it this way we killed fifty to one hundred a day."

More applause.

The killer threw his shoulders back proudly as his fellow officers patted him on the back and congratulated him for his great ingenuity.

"Turkey for the Turks," they all shouted.

I bit my lip and felt my body shake. What if they find out I am Armenian? Will they all take turns raping me after I serve the coffee? I must be crazy. Hanum would never let anything bad happen to me. She treats me like her daughter. Still, I feared for my life.

Hanum asked me to pour more coffee. Then she said to one of the men, "When Ester fully recovers, we will give her to you for marriage."

The room started to spin. I needed air. I stepped back and fell down the nearby stairwell.

Lying in a heap at the bottom of the stairs, I heard Hanum say, "Leave her alone, I'll take care of her. Come, Ester, I'll help you."

She put her arms under mine and gently lifted me. I had no broken bones, but I was shaking and crying. Hanum splashed me with cold water, helped me to my room, and put me to bed.

In the morning, I begged Yousouf Bey to take me back to Seranoush and the refugee camp.

"You mean, you want to leave the security of my home and return to the road where you will surely die?"

"Yes," I said, "I want to go back."

"Foolish girl. I won't make you stay but I will not take you back to the hills. I'll deliver you to the orphanage in Malatya."

I knew that the orphanage was located just within the Malatya city limits. *Get to Malatya,* I thought. *Sivas is due north of Malatya. If I can get to Sivas from Malatya, I'll have a straight journey north to Amasia. Yes, I must get to Malatya.*

Out loud, I said, "Please, Yousouf Bey, please take me to the orphanage."

Later that same night, word came to me by a workman that Yousouf Bey wanted to give me something for my journey the next morning.

"Follow me," he said.

I followed him out the back door to a shed behind the main house. The workman motioned me in. As I entered the small room, he spread out a rug on the dirt floor and lit a candle.

"Here, eat this candy and lie down," he said.

"But I don't want any candy," I said.

He shoved me down. "Be quiet. Hurry and eat."

I did as I was told. Soon I felt dizzy. The door opened and the shape of a tall figure in something that looked like a black cape entered the room. Darkness washed over my body. I fell asleep. When I woke, the candle was out and I was alone. The room was cold. I got up and returned to the house. Hanum was waiting for me. A warm reddish liquid seeped down along my legs.

Hanum looked at me and cried, "Oh, Ester, we didn't know you were a virgin. Come let me help you clean up. Oh, we did not know. We did not know," she repeated over and over.

She pressed her hands on my face around to my ears. She held my chin between her fingers. She stared then whispered again, "Oh, Ester, I am so sorry, I am so sorry."

I did not understand what had happened. When we were forced to leave Amasia and marched on the trail, I had stopped having my monthly bleeding. This bleeding looked the same, but I didn't have the usual stomach cramps. Was this my *amsagan* or was it something else? Yes, it was something else. I learned later Yousouf Bey had stolen my virginity. It was his parting gift to me.

Then Yousouf Bey entered the room and put a small slip of paper into my hand.

"Here," he said, "take this note and keep it with you at all times. My name is on it with the message that you come under my umbrella of safety. You may return here any time you wish and the person who delivers you will be rewarded."

I sucked my lower lip in, kept my eyes focused on the floor and held the paper tight in my fist.

The journey to Malatya took two hours by horse and wagon. A cold rain fell from the dark sky. I had a scary thought. What if there is no room at the orphanage? Where will I go then? I saw myself being thrown into a ditch to die. I pushed these thoughts from my head just as we arrived at the orphanage. It was a little after sunset. The *vorpanotz* was crammed with children of all ages. They hung out from the windows and peered from behind open doors. They all wanted to see what the new arrival looked like. A large woman with brown curls piled high on her head greeted me at the door.

"Welcome," she said. "I am Mayrig."

How many mothers would I have? First there was my birth mother, whom I never really knew. Then came Pepron who had died of pneumonia, next there was Vartouhi, who disappeared on the death march, and then Hanum who claimed she wanted me for her daughter but instead took me as a whore for her husband. Perhaps this was a bad dream. Would I soon wake and find myself in my bed in Amasia?

Mayrig took my hand, "Come, Ester. I'll show you where you will be sleeping.

We entered a room with ten beds pushed up against the far wall. In the center of the room there was a table and some chairs. Children of all ages were sweeping, making beds, and cleaning toilets in the bath down the hall.

"You will sleep with Mary and Sophia in that bed."

She pointed to a bed in the corner of the room.

A chubby girl walked toward me and said, "I'm Mary. I'm fourteen years old. That's Sophia in the bed. She's five years old and too sick to eat. Come on, I'll take you to the dining hall for dinner."

"I thought I would never see a girl my own age. Most here are younger or older than me," she told me.

We ate silently. I could feel the eyes of many in the room watching me. I wondered how they all got here. I asked no questions.

Dinner was some of the same watery broth with a couple of pieces of stale bread and yogurt as we had on the march. After the meal we went straight to bed. I pushed my body to the right side of the mattress and tried not to touch the other two. Sophia, the five year old, slept in the middle and never moved all night.

In the morning, someone said, "Sophia's dead."

Mary put her hand on my arm under the blanket and whispered, "Don't move, Ester. Someone will come and take her to the death wagon."

"What death wagon?" I asked.

"Each morning the death wagon comes to pick up those that have died during the night. Shush, here she comes."

A matron dressed in white reached over me and grabbed the dead little girl by one skinny arm. I rolled over and watched as she dragged her down the steps. The little girl's body bounced with a dull thud on each step. I watched her head flop from side to side like a rag doll. I shoved my head under the pillow and covered my ears with both hands. What a dangerous choice I had made, and I was no closer to my family. There was no hope. How long would it be before I died like Sophia?

Mary was short and very fat. She took up most of the bed and all of the covers. We both had head lice so we scratched and picked all day. We made believe the lice were our friends.

"Hello, Ester, meet my friend Kirkor," she said, as she handed me a few white flakes from her head. They flipped around in my hand. "How can I tell which one is Kirkor?" I asked.

"Oh, he's the one on the left and he itches the most."

We giggled and introduced more lice to each other.

"What happened to your family?" I asked.

"They were all killed on the road. I escaped under a wagonload of soldiers who didn't know I was hanging on to the bottom of the wagon. After I was discovered, they dropped me off here. I'm the only one left of my family."

"I think I'm the only one left of mine," I said.

She spoke in Armenian in a low whisper.

"No, do not talk to me in Armenian," I said. "You know it's against the law, and we'll be punished."

"What could be worse than this?"

"What could be worse, I'll tell you what," I said in Turkish. "You could be beaten and starved to death." She shrugged her shoulders. Her eyes showed no emotion.

She rolled over, pulled the covers over her head and muttered, "So what."

Every morning Mayrig told us the chores that were scheduled for the day. We scratched our heads and scrubbed the floors. We scratched our heads and worked in the kitchen. We scratched our heads and washed clothes. Mostly we just scratched our heads.

A week had gone by. I was alive, but no closer to Papa or Vartouhi. I wanted to believe they were still alive, too.

One day Mayrig told us to follow her into a large empty room on the third floor.

"Open all the windows, we are going to have a special bath," she said. "Take off all your clothes and pile them over there in the corner."

"What's going on?" Mary asked.

"Never you mind," Mayrig replied. "Just do what I say."

We all took our clothes off. I shyly turned toward the wall. From the corner of my eye, I saw Mayrig carry in some buckets filled with a foul-smelling liquid. She sat on a square wooden stool in the middle of the room and called us over one by one. Then she took a soft sponge, dipped it in the bucket, and squeezed the smelly water over Mary's head.

"Do not open your eyes or you will be blinded," she warned.

When it was my turn I stepped forward slowly and lowered my chin to my chest. I stared at my feet. I hated being naked. The cool liquid rolled slowly down my back from the top of my head. It flowed to the end of my nose and formed a yellowish bubble. It seeped into my ears and down my neck.

"This will ease the itch of your body rash," Mayrig promised.

"But I don't have a body rash, Mayrig."

"Well, most of the others do and soon you will too. Hush, it will also kill the lice in your head and disinfect any body germs you may have in hidden places."

What hidden places? Mayrig took her hand dipped it in the liquid and massaged between my legs and through the crack in my behind. I took a deep breath. There was a sharp sting, then a feeling I had never felt before. I sighed. Mayrig smiled.

"Now doesn't that feel good, Ester?"

My face felt hot. I didn't look up. I only whispered, "Yes, Mayrig." I didn't want the other girls to hear me.

After we were all disease-free, we returned to our lice-infested beds. When the lights went out I rolled away from Mary. I didn't want to be touched anymore.

Once a week, Turks came and took their pick of the girls. They chose as many as they wanted for cooks, field workers, housekeepers, or wives. Like slaves, no one asked any questions. No one had a choice. On those mornings, we were shoved toward the staircase in the center hall of the orphanage. At the bottom, the *zaptyiehs* separated the line into two groups. One side was for the selection of the Turks who came looking for free labor. The other side was for those not good enough for anything. They were taken a short distance away from the main building, pushed into a pit and shot. I knew this because I could see it all from my window. I wondered if I would be taking that walk soon.

For several weeks I escaped the lustful eyes of the shoppers and the death demons. Each time I went down those steps, I'd think, maybe this will be the day I'll get picked for the death line. Instead, I was marched back up the stairs under Mayrig's watchful eye.

One morning, I got pushed to the right, "Move, girl, *yallah*."

I looked up at the soldier. He was skinny, had a flat wide nose and bad skin. He looked about sixteen years old.

When he pushed me again — toward the death line — one of the girls next to me shouted, "Go ahead, Ester, show him your note. Oh, how lucky you are to have that paper. You will not be killed."

"What paper is that?" he said, as he grabbed my arm.

I took Yousouf Bey's note out of my pocket and tore it into small pieces.

"Aieee," shouted one of the girls, putting her hands over my mouth. "Don't say anything, Ester, you are crazy. You'll surely die now. You just threw away your only hope."

My eyes darted from side to side. Standing there with someone else's hand over my mouth, I wondered what to do next. I knew I wanted no part of returning to Yousouf Bey, the man who raped me.

I felt a strong yank on the collar of my dress. A rough, blistered hand circled mine and pulled me through the crowd. With one high swing, I was tossed into the back of a wagon.

ELEVEN

ROCKAWAY BEACH

MARGARET — SEPTEMBER 1998

Clutching a basket of dandelions I'd picked from my lawn, I pushed through the door of the office staff in the Armenian Home, a stop I usually made before climbing the stairs to Mother's room.

"Your mother has pneumonia," the floor nurse said. "The doctor is coming to see her later today. We think she'll be okay, but only the doctor will know for sure."

I raced up the stairs to Mother's room.

I stopped just outside her door, which was ajar. I saw Mother struggling to dress herself. She was fighting to maintain her independence. Her will was still strong. An aide arrived to help. Did she come because she saw me or would she be helping Mother even if I weren't there?

Mother saw me. "Ah hah!" she said, and put on a cheerful smile. "Come in, come in. I'm almost dressed."

"I've brought you some flowers and some madsoon abour."

"Oh, madsoon abour, I used to make that for Ronnie," Mother recalled.

I thought about my nephew Ronnie, Mother's grandson. I remembered how he loved her yogurt soup. Mother made the soup for him before he died of complications brought on by pneumonia.

Pushing this memory aside, I carefully unwrapped the foil covering from the still-warm soup and fed Mother.

"Yummmm, this is good. I feel better already. May your daughter someday feed you soup this good."

Then she pushed my hand aside. "Hand me the bowl, your spoon is too small." Mother held the bowl with two hands and tilted the container to her lips as she gobbled the soup.

"Ah, that's better. Why did you come today? Did you know I was sick? I'm so happy you're here. You know it's all from God the things that happen to us. There is nothing we can do about it. It is His will. The only thing we can do is try to be strong. Look at all the things I went through. I never complained."

She leaned towards me. "Remember one thing — Vailey — live every minute as though it were your last, and don't get fat! Listen, take care of your teeth, too, or you'll wind up with these."

Mother whipped out her full set of false teeth and shoved them under my nose. I silently vowed I'd call my dentist as soon as I got home.

Mother continued, "Keep your mind clean and think good thoughts and all will be good."

"Do you mean, be clean of body and mind?" I asked.

"Yes," she said. "But most important, be clean of heart. You know I never did a bad thing to anyone. I think that's why God protected me. We are all here to help others. Someone always helped me; you must do the same.

"You've always worked with children. This is good. It is what life is about. When you teach and help others, you grow. But you must also forgive the past. Forget it or it will eat you up. Remember, the more good you do, the more God will do good for you."

"But," I said, "what about the people who do good things all their lives and never have any good luck? Some of these poor people are plagued with a succession of continuous bad luck. And what of those who step on everyone around them to get to the top? They always seem to get more."

"God watches those people who do bad things. They are not fooling anyone. The stealers and the greedy will have things taken from them one day. It all comes back. Asdvadz keedeh — God knows," she repeated.

I wondered, how does she know that God knows? She never spoke this way before. Does one have a greater power to prophesize when one is closer to the end?

"Mother, I've brought you a basket of flowers."

"Bring them closer, I can't see. What are they?"

"Yellow dandelions," I answered.

It was the summer of 1949. Every year we vacationed at Rockaway Beach on the South Shore of Long Island. There were several families like ours who ritually returned year after year on Memorial Day, and systematically said their sad good-byes on Labor Day weekend.

Those were carefree happy days. Fireworks every Friday

night, merry-go-rounds, creamsicles, and boys. Every evening I'd wait at the bus stop for my father, who commuted from the steamy city where he worked as a drill press operator in an unairconditioned factory.

I loved waiting for Papa. He was always the first to jump off the bus. He'd grasp my hand tightly before we headed for the rooming house where we rented space for the summer. Then, without a word, we'd change into swimsuits and head for the beach. The waves were often higher than my head. Papa held me firmly. I was never afraid. With my fingers intertwined in his, I knew nothing bad could ever happen to me.

On weekends, we'd swim before breakfast, sometimes as early as 6 A.M. The water was usually cold this time of day, but that never stopped Papa. He forged right in, with me in tow. I never let on that I was freezing. I wanted to be with him.

On Sundays, we'd sit on the sofa and Papa would read me the comics. I watched his eyes skim the pages. His thinning gray hair lay flat against the sides of his narrow face. When he laughed, tiny little lines appeared around his eyes. I wondered why I didn't have these little circles, which fanned out evenly like the flow of ripples made by a rock tossed in the ocean.

Papa played pinochle all day with his male friends while Mother gossiped with neighbor ladies on nearby blankets. Mother packed our lunch, which was usually last night's leftovers between slices of thick, freshly baked rye bread. It was my job to pick up the bread each morning from Mr. Finklestein, the baker. I ate both crusty ends before delivering what was left of the middle to Mother. She'd scold me and demand I bring her home a whole loaf the next time. I'd promise I would, but never did.

Mostly I walked the boardwalk with older girls and stared at boys. The boys ignored me. I hung out on the periphery of the "in" group, hoping that some would believe I was part of the crowd.

One day I made the mistake of asking Mother if I could shave my legs like the other girls. The hair on my legs was dark and long. Mother went wild.

"You want to shave your legs? I'll tell you what will happen if you shave your legs! You'll get raped and pregnant and I'll send you to a home for unwed mothers!"

Huh, I should get so lucky. With my skinny, hairy legs, greasy hair, and pimple-covered face, I couldn't get anyone to talk to me, much less rape me. But, alas, leg shaving was not to be.

Some days, Mother and I picked dandelions in the public park, which was right in the walkway of the path to the boardwalk. I hated doing this. She'd mutter something about the vitamins in the leaves and the healthy salad they would make. The little yellow flowers would shake in my hand as though they were small live beings.

"Hurry and pick before the guard chases us away," Mother ordered.

I was too busy to worry about the guards. I hunched down low and prayed that none of my friends saw me picking dandelions for dinner.

I woke from my reverie when the floor cleaner arrived with his mop. I waited in the hall as Mother, from her bed, directed the workman about how she wanted her floor cleaned.

"You missed a spot," she said. "Here, over here with that mop."

I was amazed that in her weakened condition she was still giving directives. The cleaner silently did what Mother asked him to do.

"You know, I remember the past so well, but I can't re-member what I had for breakfast."

"Neither can I, Mother. Neither can I."

The nurse arrived and took her blood pressure. 122/80. No temperature. Mother's stats were better than mine.

"I think your mother is considerably better. Her lungs sound clear and I believe she is over the worst. The doctor will call you later with a full report," the nurse said.

"Is my mother happy here?" I asked the nurse.

"Your Mother is a people person. She would not be happy with one caretaker. She loves interacting with the other resi-dents."

Mother heard us.

"Don't worry about me, I'm very comfortable here. And after all, I'm not here forever. I'll be going home soon, right?"

I lowered my head to avoid her eyes. "I don't know, Mother" was all I could muster.

I leaned my back against the wall of her room.

Mother ignored the fact that I hadn't really answered her question. She quickly switched to the problem at hand.

"Don't lean against the cold wall, you'll catch a cold," she said.

The nurse smiled, "Perhaps that's good advice."

"Remember, too," Mother added, "always eat something before you go out. Even if it's something small. Don't go out with an empty stomach because the germs in the air will get into your belly and make you sick. If your stomach is full your body can fight off germs. It's also a good idea to have a little" she held two fingers an inch apart the size of a shot glass, "Jack Daniels. It's good for you to have a little one every day. It will keep you healthy. I always took a little bit of whiskey, now I *have none," she hesitated, "unless you have some in your purse."*

"I don't have any in my purse," I replied, wishing I had thought to bring some.

"Okay, take a deep breath. Forget the whiskey. Remember, I mean a really big, deep breath. Hold the air in your lungs until you think you can't hold it another minute, then hold it for five more seconds. Watch me."

She took in a breath that only an Olympian athlete could manage.

"Now that's how you take a deep breath," she said.

I turned to the nurse, "My mother's been practicing the breathing techniques of the Yogis all her life."

"That's probably why she is so healthy," the nurse replied.

"I'm thirsty," Mother said.

I handed her a glass of water.

"Asdvadz chour ee bez duvlet dah." May God flow abundant gifts over you like water.

I placed a pillow at her back.

"You think of everything," she said.

I wondered who did these things when I wasn't here.

"We have special entertainment today," the nurse announced. "Why don't you take your mother to the solarium? It will do her good to get out of bed."

We took the elevator to the solarium where many had already gathered. Hurrying through the back door, a thin, pasty-skinned blonde arrived carrying a keyboard. She sang Armenian songs in the style of a Portuguese Fado singer. Many sang. Some danced. Jack, a resident who has difficulty walking, was dancing. He spun around and danced up and down the aisle. It was as though once started, he clicked onto a track and couldn't stop. Like an electric train under a Christmas tree, Jack circled the room again and again. He looked a little dazed. Drool hung from his lips and his shoes had large gaps in the back. I wondered whether his feet had shrunk or if he was wearing someone else's shoes. A green "Happy Birthday" hat was perched nattily on his head.

As he passed us, Mother turned to me and said, "You know, if your Papa had lived he might have looked like that." Then, thoughtfully, she added, "Your Papa was so handsome when he died. Thank God, he didn't have to suffer this. I miss him. He was a kind man; he never once talked about the time I was married to Shamil. He knew it was a memory I wanted to forget."

Mother closed her eyes, tilted her head back, and whispered.

"I remember the first time I saw Shamil."

TWELVE

LIFE WITH SHAMIL

ESTER — 1915–1918

Tossed in the back of a wagon, I raised my head and saw Shamil's face for the first time. Shamil Durhan-Olan looked no more than eighteen. The white turban wrapped tightly around his head framed his bony young face. His deep blue eyes fixed on my face. He smiled. Then his face turned into a sneer. His mouth hardened and his eyes got very small.

In a deep voice, he grumbled, "Stay put," as he climbed up into the wagon and grabbed the reins. I was sure I was in a deeper mess than before, but I would not cry. I willed the tears not to fall. This was no time to cry. I had to think of a way to escape. Next to me in the back of the wagon was a Turkish

Army officer and his wife. I could tell he was an officer from the medals on his uniform.

I overheard him say to someone I could not see, "My wife and I are traveling to Sivas." *Sivas*, I thought, *my journey back to Amasia would be closer from Sivas.*

I crouched low and kept my eyes down. When I thought it was safe, I looked up and saw the officer's wife. She was pale and breathing with difficulty.

"She is very sick," the husband said.

Then he leaned over and stared in my face. I tried to ignore him. We rode without talking. Hours later, we came to a *khan* to spend the night. The inn was crowded. There were only two rooms available. The officer and his wife took one room and Shamil and I took the other. Shamil shoved me through the door. "Wait here," he barked.

There wasn't much furniture in the room: one double bed with a faded rose-colored bedspread and a small table jammed up against the left side of the bed. On it was a double-bulb brass lamp. One bulb was missing. A cracked mirror hung above a wash bowl on top of a chest of drawers. I looked in the mirror. My loosely braided hair hung low about my face. I was surprised to see that I looked the same.

I remembered the warning from the older girls at the orphanage. "If you are taken by a Turk, hold out as long as you can. Once they have you, they'll kill you."

I stood in the center of the room wondering what to do next. I had to escape. I leaned over and looked out the window. It was a short jump to freedom. But where would I run?

I was sitting on the windowsill ready to jump when Shamil returned. He grabbed my arm and dragged me back out to the wagon. He tossed a horse blanket over me and shoved me down. I lay there, afraid to move. Slowly he reached his hand under the blanket and grabbed my breast.

"No, please," I said, pushing his hand away.

"Be quiet, I just want to be sure you're not a boy. You're not much, but you are a girl. We've been thrown out of our room because a more important traveler has arrived. We'll have to sleep here," Shamil said. "Huh, they treat me like scum because I'm just a wagon-driver. Some day they will be sorry they did that."

I had heard that, in the Turkish tradition, before a man has sex with a woman, he must first cleanse his genitals. Luck was with me. There was no water in the wagon. Shamil would have to wait. He pushed me farther back in the wagon until my spine rested against the metal latch. He cursed the hotel people for a long while before he fell into a deep sleep. I sat rigid and watched as he slept. Each time I moved an inch, he opened his eyes and grabbed hold of my skirt. There was no escape.

In the morning, the Turkish officer and his wife returned to the wagon. The wife was now spitting up blood. Her breathing was uneven and she coughed a lot. She mumbled something about dying soon. I was too tired and frightened to listen. All day and through the next night she whispered strange things.

"You'll be all right," the husband said. "We'll be home soon and you'll be comfortable in your own bed."

She never answered him.

None of us were surprised the next morning when the officer said, "My wife is dead."

We buried her by the side of the road and continued on. I wondered why he didn't take her body to his home, if it was so close by. I asked no questions. I really didn't care what he did with her.

Soon, the Turkish officer started eyeing me, but only when Shamil wasn't looking.

The next day he leaned over and whispered, "Why do you go with him? Come with me. I live two days' journey from here in a beautiful house. My wife is dead. You can have her jewels. Here, I have some with me."

The weight of the gold he pushed into my hand fell hard in my lap. How could I go with him? If I stayed with Shamil and went to Sivas, I might find Vartouhi and Papa. I shoved the gold back at him and hissed through my teeth, "I'll tell Shamil what you said and he'll kill you." Shamil never heard us.

By day, we rode silently and at night I moved deep into the far end of the wagon away from both men. Soon we passed a group of workers walking slowly along the side of the road. I stretched my neck to see if any of them looked familiar. I knew no one. The men were connected by a thick black chain. Turkish soldiers on horseback carrying guns and swords followed close by. As our wagon passed, some turned their heads to look, but most stared straight down at the muddy dirt under their feet.

On the third day we dropped the officer near his house. He gave me one last nudge and mumbled, "Come with me, you little fool."

This time Shamil heard him. He yelled, "*Yallah, yallah,* get away from her, give me my money and go." Shamil was concerned more about his money than me.

The man left the wagon, muttering something about how stupid I was. I crouched down low once again in the back of the wagon as we headed for Sivas.

We arrived in Sivas at dusk. When we pulled up to Shamil's house, all the neighbors came out to see what Shamil had brought home.

"Ah, hah," one laughed. "Shamil has a *giavour* in his wagon."

Yes, I was his *giavour,* his infidel dog.

We entered the house. Three women came towards me. They crept closer and closer to look me over. I slowly backed away. They kept coming. Suddenly, I felt the solid surface disappear beneath my feet. I was covered with a warm sticky foam. I had fallen into the fire pit. Covered with black soot, I was a pitiful sight. There I stood, speechless, staring up from the hole. Everyone laughed.

"Look, look, your *giavour* is so stupid she has fallen into the cooking pit."

Shamil was not laughing. He reached down and dragged me out by one arm.

"You stupid pig! You stupid pig!" Shamil shouted, beating me with his fists.

Shamil's mother, Selka Hanum, caught my free arm and pulled me away from him. She took me next door, where she and her daughter and daughter-in-law lived. Shamil's screaming voice followed us, but luckily he did not.

Their house was small. A center room served as a sitting, cooking, and eating room. Off to one side were alcoves where the women slept. The furniture was worn and dirty. One worn-out rug covered the center of the dirt floor.

"Don't worry," Shamil's mother said, "he'll forget about his anger in the morning. What's your name?"

"Ester," I replied.

"Not any more," she said. "From now on your name will be *Gezeer Kateejeh.* Tomorrow we'll prepare you for your wedding."

My wedding? What wedding? I was confused. I was tired. I was hungry. Why did he want to marry me? Then I remembered the older girls talking in the orphanage about Turks marrying Armenians because it was against Turkish law to keep a refugee in their house. Turks were allowed to marry Armenians or kill Armenians, but not house Armenian refugees. The government would not know that I was a refugee from the death march. They would only know that Shamil married an Armenian pig.

Shamil's mother then said, "After you eat, you may sleep over here next to me." She pointed to two bedrolls in a corner of the room. "Heurria, bring Kateejeh some food and water."

I ate in silence. Selka Hanum told me that Shamil's brother was away at war fighting on the side of the Germans.

"We have not seen him for a long time," she said. "His wife, Herurria, lives here with us. You'll get to know her and my daughter, Meurria, Shamil's sister. She lives with us too because she is not married. We keep the houses, sell bread at market, and wait for Shamil to come home."

"Why do you live in separate houses?" I asked.

"This is our way. The three of us have always lived in this house. Shamil lives next door. You will live with him while he is in town. When he goes away for his business you will move in here with us."

The following day I woke early. After a breakfast of cheese, olives, and warm bread, Hanum cut my hair in the style of the Turkish girls, with long bangs in front. Meurria, Heurria, and Hanum cut and sewed some white material and quickly fitted the dress to my body. A tuck here and there and it was done. On my feet they put a pair of red *yemini*. The red leather slippers with turned up toes were trimmed with blue and silver bows. A veil flecked with gold covered my face. I was dressed, but not ready.

Dressed as a bride, I stared at myself in the only mirror in the house. It was hard to hold back my tears. Where was my family? Had these people I was living with killed them all? Perhaps not directly, but there was no doubt in my mind that, given the chance, Shamil would have shot them. If he hadn't chosen me from the orphanage, I, too, would be dead.

There was a loud knock at the door. It was the local Imam who came to perform the ceremony. Several neighbors came in and brought chairs with them. They formed a circle and Shamil and I stood in the middle. This Muslim priest made Shamil promise that if he ever divorced me, he would pay me a dowry of thirty gold coins. This was the traditional vow that all Turkish grooms made to their brides. Shamil smiled when he uttered this promise. He knew he would never have to pay this *giavour* anything. Some words were chanted in Turkish and it was done.

After a dinner of lamb kebab, rice, and wine, everyone left. Some time later, alone with Shamil in his house, I watched as he slowly and deliberately washed himself. I nervously sat on my heels and prayed to my God, as he kneeled toward Mecca and prayed to his.

Then he said, "All right, I've waited long enough."

He pushed me down on the feather bed. His breath smelled of garlic and whiskey. I turned my face toward the wall. My back pushed hard against the paper-thin mattress. I felt the wire mesh cutting through my skin. I held my breath. He pushed himself into me. Then, suddenly, he stopped pushing. He grunted and rolled over.

Maybe he's dead, I thought.

But then he started to laugh. "Ah hah, so you're not a virgin."

You're too late. That prize went to Yousef Bey, I thought, but I said nothing.

Before he fell asleep, he said, "Don't worry. I'll keep you for a while."

As a wagon-driver, Shamil was away on business most of the time. Shamil's sisters, mother, and I kept busy with our daily chore of selling bread at the local market. It was my job to buy the grain and take it to the mill to have it ground into flour. Then we all kneaded and rolled the dough into balls for baking. Next we took the raised dough to the baker who baked the bread for everyone in the neighborhood. The last task was to sell the bread at market. Sometimes there was a small profit left over after we paid for the grain, the miller's fee, and the baker's fee. This was the only income we had. Shamil's family was very poor. They had no *ambars* filled with dried fruits and beans as we had in Amasia. They lived from day to day on the pennies we earned at the market. We had very little meat and vegetables. Our daily diet was mostly bread and yogurt, not much different than my diet in the orphanage. I hadn't come very far.

Three times a day we faced Mecca and chanted Muslim prayers on bent knees. Before each session, in preparation for the prayers, we washed our hands, arms, legs, face and behind our ears. Hunched over on the opposite end of the room, I said my Christian prayers very low under my breath to the beat of the Muslim chant. Clenched tightly in my fist was Grand-mom's little iron cross, the one she gave me on the march from Amasia.

This worked for a couple of months. Then, one day, Hanum and Heurria suspected something. They stopped chanting and heard me praying in Armenian. They pushed me off my prayer rug and rolled me over. They demanded that I show them what I was hiding in my fist. I froze. They pulled and tore at me and pushed me against the wall. Heurria forced open my tightly closed fist and there, shining like a star, was my little metal cross.

"*Giavour, giavour!*" Heurria cried. "Such a Turk. You were only pretending to say the Muslim prayers. All the while you were chanting your Christian pig prayers. We'll tell Shamil what you've been doing when he gets back and you'll see what happens then." Selka Hanum shouted, "Go on! Get out of here."

I sat outside under a tree behind the house, waiting for Shamil.

I had a plan. I'd just hide the cross and deny the whole story. Shamil would believe me. But where should I hide it? This two-inch cross now seemed four feet long. I could not find a place out of sight. I noticed a small crack in the brick wall where the rain had washed away the mortar. I kissed my cross, wrapped it in my handkerchief, and pressed it into the tiny space. Then I gathered some mud and filled in the hole. Satisfied, I leaned back and waited for Shamil until dark.

Shamil returned later that night. Before I could tell him my story, he heard theirs. He whipped me until I bled. What a fool I was to think he would believe me and not his sisters. Every day he attacked me until my skin was raw flesh. The more I cried, the more he beat me.

He beat me for one solid week.

During these daily beatings he'd shout, "You will forget your God or die."

I sat silently and took the beatings. I chanted the Muslim prayers loudly with the rest. Then the beatings stopped. Shamil believed he had won me over to his faith.

Weeks later as we kneaded bread, Hanum said to me, "I know what you are thinking. You'll escape from us and find your way back to Amasia."

I couldn't believe it. That was exactly what I was thinking at that very moment. How could she know my thoughts? Did she read minds?

"Well, silly fool, you'll never see your Amasia again. Here take this mirror. When you can see the back of your ear, that's when you'll see your Amasia again."

Later, when no one was looking, I tried to see behind my ear. Of course, I could not. Desperate, I tried every angle I could think of, but no, I could not see the back of my ear. There was only one mirror in the house. If only I could find another mirror, I could hold one in each hand and see the back of my ear. I thought of nothing else. I was convinced that if I saw the back of my ear I would return to Amasia.

One afternoon when everyone was gone, I took a copper pot and polished it till it shone like a mirror. And then, holding it at just the right angle, I saw a tiny portion of the space behind my right ear. I knew, at that moment, I would make it home.

Two years had passed and I was no closer to Amasia. With no word from Papa or Vartouhi, maybe I was the only one of my family still alive. But then I thought, could it be they were waiting for me in Amasia?

It was a hot July day in 1917 when I put on my *burug* and headed for the market with Herurria and Meurria to sell our bread. I was seventeen years old. Since this was our only source of income, every penny was closely accounted for. The *burug's* heavy folds kept the hot afternoon sun off my body. As I moved quickly through the streets, a gentle breeze slipped under the edges of the garment, cooling my legs. I tripped often because it was hard to see through the narrow eye slits. I spoke Turkish well enough now to pass as a Turk.

When we got to the open-air market, Herurria took a stall at one end of the market and Meurria and I found a spot at the other end. We played a game of competition, whoever sold their bread first got a second piece of cheese with her dinner. I had five loaves to sell at twenty coins each for the sum of what would be one U.S. dollar. This money would feed us all for one day. If Herurria sold all of hers we had extra money for luxuries such as nuts and apricots. If we didn't sell any bread, our dinner that night was bread and yogurt.

I had sold two of my loaves when a tall Turkish woman stopped at my stall. As she talked, I noticed that her *burug* was draped over my three remaining loaves of bread. She talked on and on about nothing important: the heat, the lack of rain, and the possibility of some cool showers. Then she suddenly left.

I said to Meurria, "What was that all about? Why, she didn't even buy a loaf of bread." Then, I looked down and there were only two loaves in front of me.

"That woman stole one of my loaves, Meurria." I ran after her screaming, "Thief, thief! That woman is a thief!" I quickly caught up with her, and punched her back. "You stole my bread. Pay me my money or I will call the *zaptieh*."

She turned and looked down on me. Her nostrils got red and flared out. Through pursed lips she cleared her throat and said, "I don't have your bread. How dare you accuse me — Madame Tokay — of stealing? You little street merchant, I'll have you arrested."

Out of the corner of my eye, I saw Meurria back at the stall, shaking her head in disbelief. She knew that I was an Armenian and the punishment for accusing a Turk of anything, especially stealing a loaf of bread, was a really bad crime.

Meurria motioned for me to come back. I squinted at Madame Tokay, ignoring her loud voice. I blinked the blood from my eyes and stared at her face. I took a deep breath, threw my head back, and in my finest Turkish I shouted the worst curses I had learned from Shamil. A crowd gathered and took sides.

"Give the child her bread or pay her, you witch," someone shouted.

Encouraged by this support, I shoved her against the wall and lo and behold, the loaf of bread fell out from under her *burug*. A hush fell over the crowd. I reached down grabbed my bread, held it high over my head, and loudly said, "See, I was right, this woman stole my bread."

Then I turned and slowly walked away, sure that I had won. I held my breath, just in case a last burst of energy came from the beaten witch.

Shouts of support rose from the other girls in the stalls: "Boy, are you brave, Kateejeh. How smart you are, Kateejeh. Your voice was so loud, Kateejeh. You ran so fast, Kateejeh."

I threw my shoulders back, tilted my chin up, and marched home like a soldier having won a battle. Out of sight of the market, Heurria pinched my arm and told me that my stupid bravery could have cost them their lives.

"Do you realize that if the *zaptiyehs* found out you were an Armenian, we would have all been in trouble? You put us in grave danger."

"I'm sorry about the fuss. I wouldn't want any of you to be under suspicion," is what I said. What I thought was *Yes, I hope you all get arrested and shot.*

When we got home the girls told Hanum what had happened.

Hanum put her arm around me, "You were right to stand up for yourself, Kateejeh, but remember you did put us in danger. Never do that again."

No one told Shamil.

One morning, a few weeks later, we all woke to the sound

of roaring wind and rain pounding against the walls. The heavy gusts rattled the loose windows. Leaves blew wildly everywhere and dark clouds loomed overhead. We latched the rattling windows and doors as best we could, and sat huddled in the center of the room. The walls shook and the ground moved beneath us.

"Quick," Hanum shouted, "Get out of the house. It's an earthquake."

"What's an earthquake?" I cried.

"Soon the ground will open and swallow the house and all of us," Heurria screamed.

"Why do we want to go outside? It must be safer in here."

"No, no, quickly, you fool, get out," Hanum ordered, pushing me toward the door.

I fought as hard as I could to stay inside but the women overpowered me and dragged me out at the exact moment that the front windows and part of the front wall fell inward. I stared in disbelief. The spot in the house where I had been standing was now an eight-foot tall mound of stones and broken glass.

We pushed some of the pile aside, boarded up the windows with wood and waited for Shamil. He was no help. Whenever he returned from one of his trips, all he did was drink and sleep. We never repaired the damage; we just lived around the mound of stone. Selka Hannum reminded me that I could have died if I hadn't gotten out of the house. I was alive, but still a slave.

While Shamil was in town I took care of his every need. "Hey, *giavour,* come and rub my back. Get me some food. Clean this floor. Water my horses. Bring those packages in from the wagon. Take these packages out to the wagon."

In between trips, if I passed too close to him he would reach out and kick me. If I cried, he'd kick me again. I tried not to cry. By day, I was his slave. At night, I was his mistress, except on certain nights when he had other company.

Shamil liked to drink. He'd go to the local coffeehouse where there were dancing girls and drink most of the night. It didn't take much to get him drunk. Those were the nights I feared most. I'd go to bed early and pretend I was asleep when I heard him come in.

One night, I saw him enter the front door with his arm around a dancing girl. His body swaying and his breath full of whiskey, he shouted, "Hey, *giavour,* look what I have here."

The girl giggled. I lay still in bed with my head down.

"Come on, wake up and see what a beautiful girl looks like."

I didn't move. He stumbled toward the bed. He took off his clothes and hers and fell into the bed almost landing on top of me. Hunched in a heap, I listened to their lovemaking. I felt anger. Was I jealous? Had I come to love this animal I lived with? Why did I care that he brought another to share our bed? I turned my back to them, put my hands over my ears and cried through the night.

In the morning I came face to face with a frizzy-haired woman. Her body was covered with rolls of fat and her makeup was smeared. She smelled of stale whiskey. I turned away and busied myself making coffee. She came over and ran her hand down the side of my face.

She whispered in my ear, "Don't worry, I won't take him away from you."

It was true. I had begun to care for this terrible man. I could not understand what I felt, only that I was angry and jealous that he brought another woman to our bed. I missed him when he was away. When he returned, he beat me and cursed my ancestors. I was truly insane.

During the three years I lived with Shamil and his family, we had very little food. Turkey had joined forces with Germany against the Americans. The war had drained everyone's supplies. We never had much and now we had less than we had before. Thoughts of my family and friends dying with full stomachs filled my mind. I was alive but still hungry. These Turks I was living with were suffering too. "Turkey for the Turks" was the cry I heard in the streets of Sivas. It didn't seem like much of a victory to me.

I was now eighteen years old and Shamil and his family were all I had. I dreamed of Amasia, but only silently in my head. I could not share my thoughts and dreams with a soul. I talked to the pebbles in the street. I talked to the grain in my sack. I talked to the ovens belching out streams of hot air. I talked out loud to the lifeless objects around me. The only sound I heard was the low voice in my head and Shamil's loud shouting.

One day, I overheard some local Turks talking about Armenians.

"You know, it's only a question of time before all the Armenians are killed. By the end of this year there will be no Armenians left."

All Armenians dead? I sat alone on the floor in the creeping dusk of day. I ran my hands down my face, over my lips, and around my ears till they reached my chin. Finally I would be dead. Would it be tomorrow? Would it be while Shamil was home? Would he help them slit my throat? I sat very still.

Then, a month later, people in town whispered that the Turks and the Germans had lost the war. They said the Americans had won.

May 1918 brought news that a small group of Armenian revolutionaries had founded an independent Armenia. The

Turkish men at the coffeehouses talked about Armenian troops advancing toward Sivas to save the refugees. I had a sudden burst of hope. Could it be true? Soldiers coming to Sivas to save the refugees? Soldiers coming to save me! Shamil feared these forces so much that he made me promise to speak on his behalf when the soldiers arrived.

"You must tell them that I have been good to you, Kateejeh. You must tell them that I saved your life."

I thought, he's calling me Kateejeh and not *giavour*. He must be really worried. There was no need to worry. No troops came.

One morning late in June 1918, while I was kneading dough, I heard the sound of *davoul* and *zourna* music in the street. The steady beat of the drum mixed with the rhythm of the flute created an interesting sound. As if in a trance, I walked outside and let the music flood over my body. Not looking in either direction, I was nearly run down by a transport wagon swiftly moving down the street.

At that moment, something inside me snapped. With my hand still dripping flour and dough, I ran after the wagon. I was certain that my brother Haroutoun was in the wagon. As I ran, I thought, what am I doing? This is crazy. If I'm wrong, I'll be punished for running away, and severely beaten. But even if I'm right, and he is in the wagon, would he recognize me after all these years? The last time I saw him I was fourteen years old. That was four years ago. I'm not the innocent little girl he once knew. Logic had no hold over me. I ran. When I could not run another step, I sank to the ground, sobbing. I watched as the wagon slowly faded into the horizon. A farmer working in the field nearby asked what was wrong.

"My brother is in that wagon. I have to catch him but I can't run any more." I wiped away my tears with the back of my hand and got up to run again. The farmer cupped his hands around his face and shouted, *"Yayligee, yayligee."* His voiced echoed loudly, again and again until the wagon slowed down, then stopped.

"Go," the farmer said, "I've stopped the wagon for you."

As I got close, a man in Turkish uniform jumped down and in a stern voice asked, "Who are you? Why did you make us stop?" I raised my face to his. He looked into my eyes and a strange questioning look crossed his face.

"Who are you?" he said, lifting my chin up.

"It's me, Ester, don't you know me?"

"Oh my God, Ester, my little Ester."

He wrapped his arms around me, lifted me off the ground, and crushed my face to his chest. The cold buttons and medals cut into my skin. His rough wool coat smelled of sweat and cigarettes. I didn't care. I didn't move.

"Ester, tell me all that has happened to you. Where have you been? Where are the others?"

Another man leaned out of the wagon window and asked what the delay was about.

"Come on, let's get going," he shouted.

Haroutoun quickly wrote something down on a piece of paper.

"Meet me tomorrow at the Bagradians, Ester. Here, this is their address," he said, handing me the slip of paper. "They are friends of mine and they will help you. Be there at 2 P.M. Tell no one about this."

I ran home carrying my secret. That night I ate in silence. I cleaned up and went straight to bed. I was afraid that if I spoke one word I might blurt out my secret.

The next day, I left the house with the address hidden in my fist.

"I'm off to market," I said out loud. Since I said this every day no one suspected a thing. After I left the house, I headed toward the market. Once out of sight, I quickly changed my direction and searched for the Bagradian house. When I arrived Haroutoun was already there. He explained that the Bagradian family was leaving Sivas for Amasia and for a fee they would take me with them.

"But I have no money."

"I've taken care of everything," Haroutoun said. "Now quickly go home and tell no one of this plan. Be here by sunset the day after tomorrow."

Never knowing when Shamil would return from one of his wagon trips, I prayed to God that he would not come back for at least one more day.

THIRTEEN

EAGLE ON A PERCH

MARGARET — OCTOBER 1998

My arms were filled with perky alstromeria, a happy flower for a happy day: my birthday. I chose alstromeria for Mother because it would be a couple of weeks before I could return. These flowers were hardy, they would last longer than roses.

I quickly scaled the stairs to the second floor. Mother's room was empty. I walked quietly down the hall looking for her. In several rooms I saw the hunched-over frames of frail figures sitting in chairs waiting to be walked to the solarium. The residents, unless fully mobile, were escorted in groups of two or three by an aide.

Sunlight flickered through the Venetian blinds, creating eerie stripes across the twisted bent bodies as they sat patiently waiting for an aide. Not all were patient. Some yelled, "Hey, somebody help me!" But mostly they waited. They sat and they waited.

I squeaked open the door to the shower room and saw Mother sitting on a wooden stool in the center of the tile stall. Water fell from the tip of her head, landing on her nose, chin, breasts, and knees. To my eyes, the water fell over Mother's body in the same pattern that water cascaded down the crevices of the Frank Lloyd Wright house, "Fallingwater," in Pennsylvania. Layers upon layers of water, falling, tippling, sliding over the crags and crevices of stone, dropping from one level of the house to the next. The water pouring down from the showerhead caressed Mother's bony body in the same staccato pattern.

Mother's skin hung in deep folds. Her breasts dangled like giant loaves of French bread. I ran my hands over my breasts and down my body. How soon would it be before I looked the same as Mother? Who would be bathing me? How many would be watching?

Such an indignity. I shut the door and waited outside. When I was growing up, Mother always discreetly dressed out of my sight. I rarely saw her completely naked.

Another aide swung the door fully open and Mother saw me.

"Hi, Mother, it's October 23, my birthday. How do you feel? After all, you just had a baby at 5:30 this morning."

"Fine! I feel just fine. You were an easy delivery," she quickly responded as the aide turned off the water. The shower room was hot. I stayed in the hall while mother had her hair towel-dried. It was softer and fluffier than it was the last time I saw her. Years ago, she added a blue rinse to her hair. Now with no additives it was naturally a soft pale bluish-gray.

The floral bathrobe she wore circled her body in fluffy folds. She smiled. Her cheeks creased into deep pleats like fine linen-fold paneling. Her eyes twinkled. Her skin had a pinkish glow, no doubt from the steam of the warm shower room.

"Hey, Sandy, this is my baby. I just had her this morning. I look pretty good, don't I?"

"I thought I was your baby," the aide said, hugging Mother.

"You're my baby too," Mother said.

"Tell Sandy how I gave you your birthmark. You didn't remove it, did you? You still have it, don't you?"

I cleared my throat. "Yes, Mother, I still have it. This is a strange story and many have a hard time believing this tale." I turned to Sandy. "Well, here goes. Mother told me that in the ninth month of her pregnancy with me she was watching a passing parade, when she suddenly felt a tingling in her right hand. Somehow she knew that wherever she placed that hand the imprint of what she was looking at would be emblazoned on her unborn baby's skin. Mother was staring at a passing flag depicting an eagle on a perch. She quickly placed her right hand on her lower spine, deliberately avoiding her face or any other exposed part of her body. Yes, Sandy, I have an eagle on a perch birthmark on my lower spine."

Mother smiled, "You must be careful if you get a funny feeling when you're pregnant."

"Not much chance that I'll ever be pregnant again," I mumbled.

I kissed the top of her head and cheeks. She smelled like Ivory soap.

As we slowly walked down the hall, Mother leaned on her walker, tilted her head and nodded in the direction of the staff as though she were the Queen Mother taking a turn around Kensington Park. They clapped and returned her greeting.

"I like to say hello to all my friends."

I wasn't in any hurry. I watched Mother make her rounds, then turn towards her room.

An aide helped her dress. I could see that Mother was tiring. The exertion of the bath took most of her energy.

"Why don't you lie down for a while," I suggested.

"Oh, we're not allowed to lie down and undo the bedspread," she said.

"Well, here. Lie down and I'll cover you with this blanket." Mother slipped back and grabbed my hand. I could see that she had little energy left. The aide came in and chided Mother.

"Hey, Ester, what are you doing resting in bed?"

"I'm tired from my bath," Mother answered. "Come on, lie down beside me."

The aide leaned over and cuddled Mother. The camaraderie between these two was evident.

"You know, your mother says she knew me from another life. She says we were kouyrigs *then."*

Could this large African-American woman and my frail Armenian mother have been sisters in a former life? Could I have her warm African blood coursing through my veins? Does Mother see into another dimension with her ninety-eight-year-old eyes? I looked at the aide's round, friendly face and thought, I hope so.

"Mother, I won't be back for two weeks. Not 'til after the election in November. Don't forget to vote." Mother wasn't listening. She had dozed off.

As she slept, I remembered another visit. It was September 24th. We were hiding out in New York from Hurricane George, which was headed straight for Florida. Mother and I were sitting in the solarium, when a couple of local councilmen arrived to swear in several residents as citizens.

They swept into the room and, with the help of an interpreter, quickly swore in six applicants. Several could barely stand. They raised their arms and repeated after the councilmen, "I declare my allegiance to the United States of America. I will bear arms . . ." Laughter broke out in the room from those of us that understood English.

"Today, we have six new American citizens," he continued, with conviction in his voice. "Now don't rush on down to the draft office," he added. "I don't think you'll be called, but if America needs you, I know you will serve."

Two of the new citizens were slumped in their chairs asleep. An aide was holding up a third.

He turned to each and handed them their Certificates of Citizenship, while shaking their free hands. Several had to sit because their free hand was resting on the table keeping them upright.

Then he declared, "Now, remember, on November 3rd you must all get out and vote."

Ah yes, the old get 'em out and vote speech. They'll have to bring the ballot to these folks, I thought to myself.

Everyone who could stood up and applauded the councilmen.

"He's not a der der, why is everyone standing?" Mother asked.

"He's a politician," I said.

"Humph, I only stand for priests, not politicians," was her answer. We stayed seated.

Mother woke from her nap. She reached for a tissue to clean her glasses.

"What's wrong with these glasses? I can't get them clean."

"It's not your glasses, Mother. It's the cataracts in your eyes that are clouding your vision."

"This old age is not good," she said. "I think I'm getting old."

"Mother, you will be ninety-nine in March."

"What! Are you crazy? I can't be that old. I must be . . ." she hesitated, "well, maybe fifty-three."

"That makes you younger than me," I quipped.

"It's funny," Mother answered. "My body feels old but my mind feels like it did when I was thirty."

I understood perfectly.

"I was strong when I was young. I ran after Shamil barefooted."

"Why were you barefooted?" I asked, knowing the answer.

Mother looked at me quizzically, as if to say, I've told you this story before, why do you ask again? But instead, the storyteller in her took over.

Without hesitation, she began, "He called me giavour." She bent her head. "Yes, that's what he called me. Giavour. I was like a piece of meat to him. A worthless piece of meat. Every day he would scream, dinini siktir "I fuck your religion.""

She caught her breath. Then, slowly and deliberately, she said, "I worked hard to have a good life; it wasn't easy. When I made up my mind to do something, I just did it."

"Why did you run after Shamil?"

"Shamil was afraid of fighting in the war. He escaped from Sivas and hid from the government soldiers sent to collect the Turkish boys in the hillsides for the war effort. He ran away in the dead of night. I never heard him leave. His mother didn't tell me where he went. I really don't think she knew. But I *remembered he once told me about an aunt of his who lived two hours away by foot in the outskirts of Sivas. I ran for two hours without shoes."*

Again I asked, "Why didn't you have shoes?"

"I don't remember. I only know that I ran barefoot and my feet were cut and bleeding by the time I got there. I had no fear. After all, I had come back from the dead, what was there left to fear? I had some brains left to use. If Shamil was there, it must be a better place."

"What did Shamil say when he saw you?"

"He was startled when he saw me in the doorway. He was shocked to see me. First he welcomed me, then he smacked me. That was his way."

"He yelled, the blood draining from his cheeks, 'What are you doing here? We don't have enough food. Go back to Sivas!'

"Before I thought, I answered. 'I'll walk back to Amasia.' When he heard the word Amasia, he went crazy. His cheeks turned rosy, then a deeper red. He ran his hand through his hair as if to pull it out.

"'You'll never see Amasia again,' he shouted. 'If you run away I'll find you wherever you are, and I'll kill you.'

"I shut up. I was afraid of Shamil."

"Didn't you wonder if you would be killed on the journey back?" I asked.

"I guess I wasn't as smart as you think I was. I never questioned; I just did as I was told. Oh, every now and then I stood up for myself—like running after Shamil. But in the end I usually did what I was told. When the soldiers left town Shamil returned to Sivas.

"But he was not at home the day I escaped. I'm not sure I would have risked it if he had been."

Mother lifted her eyes to the ceiling. "Thank you, dear God. I was always lucky. God always stepped in when I needed Him. He gave me the courage to go on."

I cupped Mother's face in my hands. I closed my eyes and brushed my cheek across hers. Mother, I am glad you escaped.

FOURTEEN

THE ESCAPE

ESTER — JUNE 1918

God heard my prayers. Shamil had not returned. If he had, he would have found out about my plan, and he would have surely killed me. This was the time to run. I worried for my life, but I also worried for my brother's life. If he were caught in this escape plan, he, too, would be killed. I had to stay calm. I stared at the wind-up clock on the wall, counting each beat as it ticked away. I was afraid that Hanum and her daughters could read my mind. No one noticed a thing.

The next morning I dressed, fixed breakfast for Shamil's mother and sisters, and set out for the public ovens to bake the bread I had kneaded so carefully the night before. My Greek friend, Illeeageelen Tora Kareek, was waiting for me in the same place as always, only today was different.

I thought about the times we had talked in hushed voices about the families we lived with while we waited for the bread to bake. She, like me, had been taken in by a Turkish family when her family was killed by the government soldiers. She, like me, had been beaten daily by her captor. She, too, dreamed of escaping. During our short talks, we'd plan our escape and describe how it would be when we returned to our hometowns. I don't think either of us really believed that our dreams would come true.

When the bread was ready, I leaned over to Kareek and said, "Kareek, I'm running away today. You must not tell anyone."

Kareek hesitated then said, "Here, Ester, take these."

She handed me the two large loaves of bread she was carrying. "You'll need them for your journey," she added.

This gift she offered placed her in grave danger. If she returned to her house without bread, the Turkish family she was living with would punish her. Kareek hugged me tight. I could see she was crying.

"Please, you must promise not to tell or I'll be caught," I said.

"Don't worry, Ester, your secret is safe with me." She caught her breath, then, "Please pray that my chance for escape will come soon."

"I will, Kareek, I will."

I slipped away from Kareek and ran toward the Bagradian house. I was moving so fast that my feet hardly touched the ground.

When I reached their house, I was out of breath. Mrs. Bagradian was about Hanum's age. Her narrow face had deep lines that crisscrossed up and down like a worn map. Her eyes darted from side to side. I could see she was nervous. She motioned for me to follow her back to a small shed behind the house where they kept chickens.

"Ester, stay here and be quiet. As soon as Shamil's family discovers that you have escaped, they will come looking for you. Because we are Armenian they may come here, so be very quiet. I'll bring you some food and water later, when it's safe."

"I have some bread a friend gave me. Here, you keep one." I handed Mrs. Bagradian one of my loaves of bread.

Later that night, as promised, Mrs. Bagradian brought me some chicken soup and cheese. "No one has come looking for you yet, but we must be careful; you must stay here tonight," she said.

I tore a piece of bread from my loaf and ate as though I had never eaten before. I was free of Shamil and his family; even the air seemed fresher. Filtered through the darkness, a full moon smiled down over my little shack. An owl sat perched on a limb. There was no sound.

By dawn, just as Mrs. Bagradian thought, Shamil's mother pounded on the Bagradians' front door.

"Is Gezeer Kateejeh here?" she shouted at Mr. Badgradian.

"No, we don't know any Gezeer Kateejeh. Go away," he said, and shut the door in her face.

From a crack in the chicken coop I could see what was going on and heard the conversation clearly.

"You know, if you are caught with a refugee in your house, you will be shot!" she screamed at Mr. Bagradian.

"Is Ester here," she shouted. I was surprised she called me Ester, the name I said was mine before she changed it. It was several years ago and I thought she had forgotten. Through the closed door, I heard him say, "Oh, go away, old woman, and leave me at peace. There is no one here called Gazeer Kateejeh or Ester. Go look elsewhere."

Hanum turned, scratched her head, mumbled something, and left.

The Bagradian family had survived the genocide because they were blacksmiths. The Turks had a policy of keeping a craftsman for each necessary trade in each town. There were several blacksmiths in Sivas before the massacres. I don't know why, but the Bagradians were the lucky ones chosen to live, while the rest of their Armenian neighbors were marched out into the desert. The price they paid for this good fortune was never to speak the Armenian language and never to practice their Christian faith.

I sat on the floor of the Bagradians' shed and sang songs to the chickens. The chickens stared at me as I sang my choir hymns. Then a horrible thought came to me. What if Haroutoun doesn't come back? Where would I go? I pushed the thought from my head and sang more hymns. Hanum did not come looking for me again.

On the eighth day, Haroutoun returned. I must have looked very scared because he kept telling me not to worry.

"Don't worry, Ester, we'll make it safely to Amasia. I am with you. You will never be alone again."

I looked at my brother and, for the first time in a long while, I felt safe.

In the dead of night, the Bagradians packed their household goods into a small wagon. Having only the clothes on my back, I didn't have to worry about packing.

Haroutoun stored some dried fruits and nuts in the wagon along with a small bag of his clothing, and we started our journey to Amasia. I lost one of my worn-out shoes hurrying out of the city. I tossed the other shoe by the side of the road and walked barefoot in the cool, soft mud beside the main road.

The Bagradians had one sick-looking horse to pull the heavy wagon loaded with their belongings and another horse to carry their daughter, Varsinig. Mrs. Bagradian, her husband, my brother, Haroutoun, and I walked. We walked for seven days and nights. We once had a pig in Amasia that went wild. Varsinig had the same glassy look in her eyes as that pig.

Several times, Mrs. Bagradian said, "Varsinig, let Ester ride for a while."

Varsinig answered in a loud squeaky voice, "No, no, I won't get down. I don't have to, let Ester walk. She has no right to make me share."

I prayed she would fall off and break her big fat neck. She didn't.

The walk was long. All we had to eat were the dried fruits and nuts Haroutoun had packed along with some hard bread and a few pieces of cheese the Bagradians brought along. I thought of Kareek at the bakery. I could almost smell the warm bread. Did I make a mistake? Should I have stayed in Sivas? I quickly pushed these thoughts from my mind. I must return to Amasia.

At night, we stopped by the side of the road and slept piled in clumps. Haroutoun wrapped his army coat around my shoulders like a blanket. As darkness closed in, a gathering of fireflies spun a web around us. The moon lit up our pitiful campsite with warm glowing shadows. How small and alone we seemed. It was as though we were the only people left in the world. A soft breeze ruffled the trees. I heard dogs barking nearby, but no human sounds except Haroutoun's loud snoring.

On the seventh day Amasia came into view. My feet were so thickly callused, the soles looked like old leather, wrinkled and hard. I no longer felt pain or the need for shoes. As we entered the city limits, I looked left and right for a familiar face. There was none.

It was Sunday, but there were no church bells ringing. Only the constant tipping of the water wheel, tip, tip, tip, to remind one of passing time. A heavy silence hung over the streets like a dark cloud. There were no children in sight. Also missing was the sound of marching soldiers who had filled the streets the day we left in haste three years ago. As we passed my house I noticed that it looked empty. In my mind, I truly believed that everyone was still living in Amasia but me. I thought that when I returned, neighbors and friends would be waiting for me.

But there was no music, no party, and no welcoming committee. I was returning to the scene of a violent crime. The blood had been cleaned up and the bodies taken away, but the sight of that horror was carved in my brain. I could see it all again, clearly.

"Remember the first time I saw you in that house four years ago?" Haroutoun asked.

His words surprised me. I turned and said, "Of course I remember. You were so handsome. I was so proud to learn that I had a brother like you. Was it only four years ago?"

"Yes," Haroutoun answered. "So much has happened since that day. So much needless killing. Tell me about your march from Amasia. Tell me about the Ahronians. Do you know if any of them are alive?"

As we wound our way through the streets of Amasia I explained what I had seen and lived through. He shook his head in disbelief.

"And you survived! God must have a special purpose for you in life. Yes, he surely must have placed His hand on you, my little sister." Haroutoun tapped the top of my head gently with his palm. "How does it feel to return from the dead?"

I thought for a moment before I answered. "I can breathe. The air does not smell. I have no blood or slime on my body. I can walk. I can talk. I wish I could forget. That's how it feels to return from the dead."

We came to a crossroad. It was time to thank the Bagradians for hiding me in their home for a week and for allowing us to travel with them. I stared at Varsinig and thought, *I hope you fall on your ugly face.* Out loud I said, "Thank you, Varsinig." I hoped she knew I didn't mean it.

After the Bagradians left, Haroutoun led me to a small house halfway up the street.

"Come, Ester, we're going to Uncle Karamanian's house. He'll take care of you now. I have paid him a handsome sum of money to keep you till I get back. I must return to my regiment. I'll return soon. My dear Ester, you are back in Amasia as I promised you would be."

The Karamanians were waiting for us when we arrived.

"Shhh, Shhh, come in quickly before anyone sees you," Uncle said.

Haroutoun leaned over, "No, I have no time to come in. I must leave. Remember, Ester, I'll be back soon and together we'll sail to America. There we will be safe; our lives will be different. Come, give me one last hug."

I pressed my nose against his neck, wrapped my arms around his shoulders, and thought about the far-away land of America.

I never saw my brother again.

The Karamanians had two children — a boy, Arslen, about five years old and a daughter, Nartouhi, just two. I sat nervously on the very edge of the sofa in the small living room.

The family stared at me as I gripped my hands hard and bit my lip. Then little Nartouhi came close and put her head in my lap. She opened my fist and put her chubby little hand in mine. I smiled for the first time in a long while. The boy fiddled with his nose, then stuck his tongue out at me.

"Come, let's have something to eat," Uncle said.

We moved to the dining area where I sat quietly with Nartouhi on my lap. I ate little.

"What's the matter, Ester?" Mrs. Karamanian asked. "Are you sick?

"No," I stuttered. I didn't want them to know that I was terrified, thinking about Shamil's vow to find me and kill me if I escaped. My breath came in short spurts and my chest was hurting. I didn't want to share my thoughts. My mind and my secrets were the only things that truly belonged to me. I swallowed hard and kept silent.

When dinner was over, Mrs. Karamanian led me to a room at the back of the house.

"You'll sleep here, Ester," she said.

The room seemed empty. There was one single bed covered with a faded floral bedspread. The dusty wooden floor was covered with a dirty worn-out rug. The single window in the room was open. I took a deep breath. The cool evening air helped clear the musty odor that filled my nose. Against the opposite wall there was a narrow closet with two blue sweaters and one black coat hanging side by side. On the floor was a worn pair of men's slippers next to a highly polished pair of black boots. Since I had only the clothes on my back, I had nothing to unpack.

I sat on the edge of the bed and looked out the window. I stared at the house next door. There were missing bricks, broken windows, and big hanging wooden planks ready to fall off.

The grass was brown and trampled flat. It was June but there were no flowers in bloom. A blanket of heavy fog was rolling in. My shoulders slumped low, almost touching my waist. I was worn out from the long trip. The room was cold. I shut the window and rubbed my hands together. Through the closed door, I heard Uncle and his wife arguing.

"You know, if we are caught with a refugee in our house we could be in big trouble. She has no right to put us in this danger."

Mrs. Karamanian talked over him. "But we just promised her brother we would take care of her until he returned."

"Well," Uncle said, "we'll put her in the basement where no one will see her, until I can think of something else."

I pulled the dirty, worn bedspread back and laid my tired body out flat. There was a candle on the nightstand but no match to light it. I'll just sleep through the dark of night. When the sun comes up I'll be able to think more clearly. The bed was hard, but much softer than the dirt road I had slept on for the last seven days.

In the morning, Mrs. Karamanian apologized as she pointed to the open hatch that led to the cellar. She handed me a thin brown blanket and a pillow without a pillowcase, two pieces of bread, and one piece of soft cheese.

"Here, Ester, take these with you. I am so sorry," she said over and over.

Little Nartouhi pulled on my sweater and clung to my skirt. She wanted me to carry her to the cellar. Mrs. Karamanian tore the crying child from me and loudly slammed the hatch down.

It was dim and musty down there. As my eyes got used to the dark, I found my way to a corner that was drier than the rest of the muddy dirt floor. Huddled against the cold stone wall, I cried and tried to remember what bad thing I had done in my life to deserve this punishment.

I was allowed up into the living area only at dinnertime or to use the outhouse at the rear of the house. Every night Uncle lowered the windows, and covered them with rugs before he lit the candles. He said he was afraid that his Turkish neighbors might see me and report him to the authorities.

Little Nartouhi giggled and pulled on my hair. She sat on my lap and stroked me. Her tiny fingers gently ran over every inch of my face. She stuck her little thumb in my mouth. I instinctively sucked it.

Each night I sat quietly, ate quickly, and returned to the cellar. Auntie gave me a small candle that I kept lit most of the time because it kept the rats away. There were many small rats in the basement. At first the light kept them at bay, but soon enough they edged toward me and climbed over my legs and arms. I kept shaking them off, but they kept coming back. I wanted to scream, but no sound came out of my mouth as the furry things crossed my damp skin. I pulled the thin blanket over my head and arms so that only my legs were exposed to the licking and scratching of the little beasts. If only Arsen were here, he would snap their hairy necks. Poor Arsen. I wondered if he were dead. I wondered if anyone had buried him as we had buried others. I hoped no one had eaten his flesh as he had feared.

Through the cracks in the floorboards I could hear visitors. I recognized the voices of Armenian neighbors I once knew, speaking Turkish in the living room above my head, as I sat folded over against the moldy cellar wall.

The next morning, I wanted to tell Auntie that there were rats down there but I was so afraid she would throw me out for complaining I said nothing.

A few nights later, during dinner, I asked Uncle Karamanian why he and his Armenian neighbors didn't speak Armenian in the safety of his home.

His face got beet red and he yelled, "You think you are special returning here. Well, you will not endanger us by speaking Armenian in this house. You know it is against the law. Do you want to get us all killed? Remember, stupid girl, you fell in 'black dye' and you will never be pure again." It was an old adage that if one slept with the enemy it was said that they had fallen in black dye.

What was he talking about? Was I blackened and not pure because I marched out of Amasia instead of becoming a Turk? I could see that he really didn't want me around. Poisoned by the "black dye" of sleeping with a Turk, even though it was against my will, was more than he could stand. I clenched my fists tight. I was mad.

Early the next morning, before anyone was awake, I pushed open the rusty latch on the cellar door and quietly crept out of the house. I ran down the street to my old house. The hemlocks had grown so high that they created a wall in front of the house. The house that had always been in view from the street was now hidden. The shade cast across the entrance was dark and threatening. There was a dirty cloth tossed by the door. In the past I had always wiped my shoes before entering. I reached down and slid the muddy rag over my blackened feet — old habits were hard to break. I walked through the empty rooms, remembering the happy moments of my childhood.

I sat alone on the packed dirt under the mulberry tree in the courtyard. The mulberries were hanging in thick bunches over my head. These were the same berries I had picked for my after-school snacks. The sun was shining through the leaves and cast lovely patterns on the ground around me. I reached up and filled my mouth with the delicious fruit. It tasted the same. Truly God was in his heaven but what hell was I in? How could things be so different yet still look the same? I was alone. I was afraid.

Just then I heard a noise coming from the next room. "Who is that, who's there?" I said. A Turkish woman came out from behind the curtain near the door. I looked carefully. Could it be? Yes, she was wearing my tan wool coat, the one I had left hanging behind the door the day we left Amasia.

"That's my coat you're wearing," I said. She turned and slowly walked towards me. "Look, look, and there hanging on the clothes line, my *zeirees* — school bags; they are mine too," I said. "See, there's my name, Ester, embroidered in the corner."

"Be quiet," she hissed. "I know who you are, you Ester you. You once lived here but now you are nothing but a re-turnee and if you are caught you will be arrested. You have no rights. I'm leaving, so you can have your house back but I'm taking everything in it with me. If you make a fuss, I'll have you arrested."

I stepped out of her way. She brushed past me and continued loading her wagon with the contents of my home. The pots that Pepron used to cook our meals. The silver chest, the candlesticks, my *yorghan,* and the carved wooden chest filled with the linens I had embroidered at school for my wedding day. All our thick colorful rugs were rolled up and layered in the back of the wagon.

"I'm leaving now. Get out of my way, you Armenian pig, or I'll run you over."

I was frozen in place as I watched the wagon move slowly away. Soon it disappeared around a street corner. I stepped back and I wondered if she had found Grandmom's secret hiding place. I slowly walked to the corner of the courtyard where our gold and jewels were buried. I sat down over the hiding place and dug my fingers deep in the soft dirt beneath me. Yes, the top of the metal box hit my nail. I quickly removed my hand and sat up straight. My heart was jumping out of my chest. I could not dig the box up. But why? It belonged to me and there was no one around.

I smoothed and patted down the soil where my finger had just made a hole, and slowly backed away.

I sat there for a long while, staring at the ground. I thought about Papa and our walks home from school. Suddenly, I had an idea. Maybe there would be someone I knew in Papa's butcher shop who could help me. I brushed myself off and headed toward the store. When I entered the shop I was surprised and shocked to see Papa standing behind the counter.

"Hello, Ester," he said.

"Oh, Papa, Papa! I'm back, and you were here all along." I ran to him and put my arms around his waist. I fell as I grabbed the empty air. He was gone. What a nasty trick. Papa never played mean tricks on me. I shouted again, "Papa, Papa! It's me, Ester! Where are you?"

"I'm here," Papa's voice said. Behind the counter with his arms outstretched was Papa. I climbed over the counter and fell against the far wall.

Papa was gone. The sight of the store as it was three years ago was gone. Dirt and dust covered the counters and broken glass was scattered everywhere. The stalls were empty. I had imagined it all.

"I miss you, Papa," I said to the emptiness around me.

I returned to my house and spent the next two days and nights under the branches of the mulberry tree in the courtyard. No one knew I was there. The Karamanians did not look for me. They were happy I was gone. At night I lay awake staring at the sky. The sapphire blue sky, dotted with specks of white, pink, and yellow, covered me like a blanket. I never went near the box in the courtyard floor or Papa's shop again. It was June, 1918.

On the third day, tears streaming down my face, I walked to the home of my distant cousin, Bedros Effendi Zovickian, and his German wife, Frau Gretel.

Gretel squeezed me to her chest and whispered, "Ester, you cannot stay in that house alone. It is not safe. Stay here with us. I promised your brother when I saw him last that I would take you in if for some reason you left the Karamanians." Then she added, "Listen, Ester, if you stay in that house and young Turk men find you, they will have their way with you. You'll be safe here with us. You can be my housekeeper and baby-sitter for my children."

I shrugged my shoulders. I couldn't run any more.

Cousin Bedros Effendi was the town pharmacist and an important member of the community. Each night, Turkish politicians visited as I watched from behind the heavy drapery. No one knew the Zovickians were harboring a returnee. Later, they explained me as a cousin from a neighboring town. No one questioned Bedros Effendi.

My daily chores included light housekeeping and some cooking. Most of the day I took care of Eva and Sophia, the two younger Zovickian children. The Zovickians also had one son, Aram, who was about my age, eighteen.

Within a month of my arrival I overheard Gretel whisper to her husband, "I think Ester might be pregnant by that Turk she was living with."

I listened by the door shaking with fear. Could it be true?

Oh God, please let it not be true. I did not want to have Shamil's child.

"How do you know?" he asked.

"Well, I noticed this past month she did not have her *amsagan*."

"We must ask her," he said. "Ester, come in here."

I entered the room, taking each step as if it were my last. They were both sitting on a small settee by the window with the afternoon sun at their backs. Their silhouette cast a dark shadow across the colorful Persian rug. I felt my throat tighten.

Gretel said, "Ester, we must ask you a question. We noticed that you did not have your *amsagan* this month. We are worried that you might be pregnant."

I sucked in my breath. "I stopped having my *amsagan* after the first attack, when we left Amasia three years ago."

Gretel and Bedros Effendi both leaned back and sighed. They realized I hadn't gotten my period because of the stress of the terrible things I had lived through and not because I was pregnant. The very next day, Bedros Effendi mixed a thick liquid and told me to drink it quickly. It tasted very bitter. I got my *amsagan* a few hours later and every month after that. I'm not sure that they did me a favor; this bloody thing was disgusting.

I shared many happy moments in the Zovickian household during the two years I lived with them. One day, their son, Aram, bought a sick horse from one of the soldiers marching through town. He paid very little money for the horse and nursed it back to health himself. He named the horse Gennan. Oh, how I loved Gennan. She was black and white, and fifteen hands high. I remembered my horse, Aragats. Who was riding him, I wondered. A Turkish officer? Or was he pulling a wagon for hire? Aram pulled me up behind him and wrapped my arms around his waist. Aram's body was hard against mine. I stopped thinking of Aragats and where he might be. I was riding again and that's all that mattered.

I thought of Shamil. Shamil? Was he still searching for me? If he found me, would he kill me as he had vowed or was there some thread of compassion in his heart for his *giavour*? When thoughts of Shamil entered my head, I'd wave my hand in the air, as if to wipe out the image of him. Then I'd say aloud to no one in particular, "Huh, he's probably back at the orphanage picking himself out a new girl. Just like going to the market for a new cow, only this cow cost nothing."

Gennan flew over the rocks and dirt trails so fast that his feet barely touched the ground. His tail flew in the wind, and smacked across my back. The sand kicked up behind us in a curling cloud of dust. If only I could run as fast as Gennan. But where would I run? My chay-bashi, yes, that's where I'd go. No one would find me in the orchards. Maybe Aragats was there at the *aikee* waiting for me. I pushed all thoughts of running away out of my mind. Here in the Zovickian household I was finally safe. I even had new shoes.

Amasia was the same, only the people were different. Turkish families lived in the houses of the Armenian families who never returned. Those Armenian families that remained in the city spoke only Turkish. All the Armenian churches were boarded up and stood as empty shadows against the clear sky. Did God wonder where His disciples prayed, now that their houses of worship were closed? Did He hear the Muslim chants of victory over the infidel Christians? Did He wonder where His congregation had gone? Why didn't He stop the killing? Surely He could have.

Papa's words came to me: "Ester, we must never question the message that God sends us, for with each step backward there is a hidden step forward. You may not see it but trust me, it's there." I missed Papa.

Important Turkish officials came to visit the Zovickians, but no one talked about "the trouble". It was as if it never happened. In the privacy of their homes, Armenians whispered the ugly stories, but not very often. *Mortseer* became the word they all used. But how does one forget? Those who stayed in Amasia never saw what happened on the road to hell. It is easy for one to forget what they never saw. No amount of talking could describe the pain I had lived through.

Mortseer, I'd whisper to myself again and again, hoping I could forget.

One day, an invitation was delivered. The Zovickians were invited to Manoushe Hovsepian's wedding and I was included in the invitation. Manoushe was marrying the son of a prominent Turkish family. The night before the wedding, Gretel and I went to the bride's house for the *henayeum,* the placing of henna on the bride's hands and feet to make her more beautiful for her husband.

When we arrived, all the women from the bride's and groom's families were already there. Everyone was there except the bride. After we were all seated and served food and drinks, the handmade linens from the bride's wedding chest were shown to all. Each garment was passed from hand to hand and examined for the delicacy of the embroidery, the quality of the lace, and the type of stitches used. The bride's mother chose a few pieces of clothing from this pile and took them to another room where she helped her daughter dress.

When Manoushe came out, she stared at the floor. Eyes lowered, she slowly made her way across the room. She kissed her mother-in-law's hand, her sister-in-law's hand, and to my surprise, Gretel's hand. I sat up straight and pushed my hands under me. She wasn't going to kiss my hand. We sang some songs, and had more food.

I watched closely as the women mixed the henna. The bride's mother carefully painted Manoushe's fingernails and toenails with the henna dye, then wrapped them in clean, white gauze. She was then put to bed; tomorrow was her wedding day and she needed her rest. Shortly after this all the guests left. At the same time this was happening, the male relatives of both families took the groom out and roughed him up. They pushed and shoved him to remind him that this was his last night of freedom. I didn't understand why they needed to punish him this way.

It was hard for me to sleep that night. I thought of my own wedding and the beautiful handmade clothes I would never wear. I thought about the henna that Vartouhi would never put on my hands and feet. Vartouhi, where are you? I wept. At the foot of my bed slept Misgar, the Zovickians' dog. Every time I cried, tears seemed to fall from Misgar's eyes too.

Gretel told me she had adopted Misgar when the family he lived with was massacred in 1915. A neighbor told Gretel that Misgar had witnessed the killings. Was this dog crying because he felt sorry for me? Or was he crying because he remembered the killings? Do dogs remember? Do dogs cry? I hugged Misgar and our wet faces stuck together. He licked my tears. I wiped his eyes.

The next morning, before the wedding ceremony, our family was invited to the house of the bride.

"Why is she wearing that heavy veil over her head? I can't even see her face," I said to Gretel. "Look how hard she is crying. Isn't she happy she's getting married?"

"Of course she's happy," Gretel said, "but she cannot

show her joy, she must weep in homage to her family and sit slumped over to show humility to her in-laws."

It didn't make any sense to me. We followed the parade to the Muslim altar where the groom and the Imam waited. It took several people to help Manoushe climb out of the wagon. Someone in the crowd said her beaded dress weighed more than twenty pounds. She also wore thick gold bangles on her ankles and wrists. Around her head she wore a wide mesh headband that dangled with large gold coins only an inch apart. I was sure she would fall over carrying all that weight, but she didn't. Every time she sat down or got up, two people had to help her. She looked uncomfortable. Sitting on hard pieces of metal must have been painful.

The ceremony was long. I wondered if the long sermon was preparing the couple for a long and boring life together. As these thoughts entered my head, I quickly giggled them away. Such silliness! Why should it take so long to get married? After all, the Muslim ceremony Shamil and I had took only minutes.

Next came the speeches by the in-laws. Each family praised the goodness of the other. They talked on and on about how lucky they were to have found each other.

Later, everyone went to the groom's house for dancing, wine, and food. The party went on all night and into the early morning hours of the next day.

By noon, the neighbor ladies anxiously awaited news of the marriage bed. This news was announced only if it was good.

As we hurried down the street towards the groom's house, I asked Gretel, "What happens now?"

"The groom must show his mother proof of Manoushe's virginity," Gretel said.

"How?" I asked.

"In the center of the marriage bed there's a white silk cloth trimmed with lace. After the groom and Manoushe have been together in bed, the groom presents the cloth to his mother. If it is not stained with blood, Manoushe will be shipped back to her family in disgrace.

When we arrived at the groom's house, many people were in the street clapping. The groom was dancing around in a circle waving the bloodstained cloth like a flag of victory. We, too, clapped happily for Manoushe and her honor.

Two years later, in the spring of 1920, word spread through town that the Turkish government was killing Armenians again. Even though the Zovickians had survived the first purge and their position in town seemed safe, they decided it was time to leave. Gretel asked me if I wanted to marry the young Turkish neighbor's son for safety or escape with her family to America. I could use the passport of her deceased daughter, Margaret.

"Give it some thought," Gretel said.

I sat on the damp grass behind the house and thought it through. Would I be safe in America? What would my future be? I looked over to the house next door and saw the young, pimply-faced boy. At that moment I knew I could not bed down with another Turk. "Not in this lifetime," I told myself.

Gretel's words were fresh in my ears. "Escape with us to America." I remembered Papa's disappearance, Grandmom falling under the rifle butt, Arsen taken in the night, and Vartouhi marching along without me. I'd had no word from Haroutoun for two years. If he was alive he would have been back for me. It was time to accept the fact that my family was all dead.

Then what was I leaving behind? The hunger and starvation? Shamil's beatings and abuse? The dead bodies floating in the Euphrates? The broken bodies of babies in the trenches? The sickness and disease? Sometimes, at night, in the darkness of my room, I could hear the crying of the starving children begging for my help, the help I could not give them.

I found Gretel in the kitchen paring some apples. Before she could turn around, I said firmly, "Yes, I'll go with you to America." Gretel held out her arms.

As Ester, I died that spring morning in 1920, but a new bold and grateful Margaret was born. The only thing I brought with me to America was my memory — the thing I most wanted to leave behind.

FIFTEEN

DINNER WITH A TURK

MARGARET — NOVEMBER 1998

"Mother, I brought you a water lily. Be careful you don't spill it," I said as I placed the water-filled container in her lap.

"Look, look how it floats!" Mother said.

She stared for a long time at the lily, then at me, before she spoke.

"A Chinese lady once told me that these flowers bud in the mud at the bottom of a pond and only flower when they come to the surface. I'm a little like this flower. I was so deep in the mud of sickness and death, it's a miracle I bloomed at all." She paused. "I came to America, but before I die, I wish I could go home."

Then she turned to me and said, "Why not? Let's go! Let's go find my house!"

"Mother, it's not safe for us to search for your property in Turkey. Besides, how would we find the house? It's been so many years!"

"I could find it, don't you worry. It's easy. Just ask anyone in the Savaieet Armenian sector for Bedros Effendi's house. Then cross the canal in front of his house and you will be facing the front door of my house."

Should I tell Mother that Ali, the Turkish diplomat I met in the 1970s, warned me never to visit Amasia alone? He said it wasn't safe for Armenians.

Before I could answer, she changed the subject.

"That's enough talk." she said, "Let's have lunch!"

As we waited for the elevator to take us to the dining room, Mother started singing. Aghvor atchig hos yegour indzee meg batcheeg ma dour — Nice young girl come here and give me just one kiss.

An elderly man, also waiting for the elevator, sang the next line. Now they were a duet. Then Mother raised her arms in Armenian dance mode. The man clapped. She swayed back and forth. The elevator doors opened and broke the spell. I desperately wanted to believe that Mother was happy in this place.

As we sat in the dining room, I helped her remove the tightly sealed cellophane wrappers over the salad and dessert plates. I cut Mother's meat and potatoes into small pieces.

"Here, have some!" she said, pushing a forkful of food toward my face.

"No, thank you, I'm not hungry."

She turned her head in my direction, and mouthed the Turkish words, "Biri yer biri bakar, kiyamet ondan kopar."

"What does that mean?" I asked.

"When one eats and one watches, that's how a fight starts," she giggled, punching the air with her tiny fist.

I turned my head toward some nearby noise. I noticed two residents speaking loudly to each other. They seemed to be arguing about something. Their voices got louder.

Mother and her fellow diners ignored this minor ruckus, and with their heads down, continued to eat. They pretended it wasn't happening. I was uncomfortable.

Later in Mother's room, I asked her how she was able to ignore the scene in the dining room.

"I don't pay any attention to it," she said. "One must not always see everything. There are many things these eyes have seen, sometimes it's best to be visionless. You will see many things in your life. You must not pay attention to them all."

Mother heaved a deep sigh.

"When the soldiers came, we were not ready. They swung their swords over their heads and rode into the crowd. We were only women, children, and old men. They trampled us into the dirt. I can still hear the screams."

A tear slid down her cheek. I reached for her and gently tapped her neck.

"I know I've always told you to get rid of bad memories. And I do try, but sometimes . . ." she hesitated and shrugged her shoulders, "sometimes the bad memories come back anyway. It's like a wound, if you cut your hand with a knife it bleeds, a scab forms, and then a scar. You forget the wound from time to time, but the scar is always there. It never goes away."

Mother closed her eyes. While she rested, I asked myself: Why do I keep mulling over this trauma in her life? Could it be that I had lived with this story for so long that I was enjoying

*the act of fearing and hating Turks? Could it be that I was un-
able to let it go, to turn my attention away? Swivel. Swivel. The
cataracts in the eyes. These clouds could be a blessing. I was
starting to see that.*

I remembered the first time I met a Turk. It was the 1970s and
I was living and working in New York City. As a volunteer, I
accompanied visiting ambassadors and diplomats and their
families to museums, historical sites, and social functions
during their stay in the city.

One evening, Amy Greene, my friend who was chairman
of our volunteer group, had a cocktail party in her apartment.
I think her plan was to introduce me to a friend of hers. I was
single then. Shortly after I arrived, I noticed an attractive man
moving toward me.

Amy stepped in and said, "Margaret, I'd like you to meet
Ali. He's a visiting diplomat from Turkey."

I tenuously extended my hand and said, "It's nice to meet
you," and quickly moved to the other end of the room before
he could speak. A Turk. I felt fear and anger. I wondered, why
do I always feel this way? I was born in the United States. This
man doesn't know me or the fact that I'm Armenian. Could he
tell? Does he know?

I spent the rest of the evening chatting with Richard Den-
ton, who had once been a foreign news correspondent and
knew more about Armenian history than I did. Richard had
spent some time in Turkey and Western Russia. He knew the
Armenian tale of persecution and had witnessed firsthand the
reconstruction of Soviet Armenia. I could feel Ali's eyes on
me, as I deliberately kept Richard engaged in conversation. We
discovered we had a mutual friend, S. J. Perelman, and we
swapped Sid stories for a long while. I learned that Richard and

Sid had often talked about the Armenian genocide, just as Sid and I had. I was pleased to make this connection between two intelligent men, both non-Armenian yet so well-versed in Armenian history. At one point, Richard said, "Margaret, did you know that the man across the room is a Turkish diplomat? He hasn't taken his eyes off you since you arrived."

"Yes, I do. And I'm a little uncomfortable. In fact, I think I'm going to leave now. I'll call you tomorrow."

As I was leaving, Richard promised to give me his own first-edition copy of Sid's book, Acres and Pains.

"Sid will be happy to know you have it," Richard said.

I thanked him and promised I'd call Sid first thing in the morning to set a date for the three of us to have lunch. I quickly headed for the door. I didn't want to run into Ali, the diplomat, again. I was aware that he had kept me in his sight all evening.

But as I made my way toward the door, Ali called out, "You're not leaving, are you?" I kept on walking.

I got into the elevator. It was hot. Just as the doors were closing, Ali squeezed through. I was alone with a Turk. I scrunched my shoulders, hoping to quell the rapid beating of my heart. My breath came in short spurts. Beads of sweat formed on my forehead. Why was I so afraid?

Ali casually leaned against the back wall of the elevator. "You've been avoiding me all evening. Is there something wrong? Perhaps we could have some coffee? I would like that."

He was terribly handsome. Shamil, Mother's captor, came to mind. He, too, was handsome. Could he be related to Shamil? I threw my shoulders back and loudly declared, "I am an Armenian!"

Then the elevator doors squeaked open. We were in the lobby.

"That's wonderful," he said. "We'll have much to talk about. Please join me. You don't hate me because I am a Turk, do you?"

I moved closer to the doorman for security and said, "I don't hate you because I don't know you, but I do hate your people for what they did to the Armenians." How brave I felt as I moved closer still to the doorman, who looked at me strangely. If he had been sitting down I would have been in his lap.

"Please let me explain my side of the story. What happened to the Armenians in Turkey is something I'm not proud of. My father helped many families escape during the pogroms. I'd like to tell you about him."

Sure, I thought, every German had a relative who helped Jews escape. He's so well-versed about his history and I'm so weak about mine.

I shocked myself when I said, "Yes, yes, let's do have some coffee and dessert at the Rainbow Room. I'll call a friend to join us, if that's all right with you." He'll never do it, I thought. I'll be safely out of here in just a minute.

He smiled, tilted his head to look at me more closely, and whispered, "If you feel better with a friend along, please invite anyone you wish. I just wanted to be with you a little longer and if that's what it takes, so be it."

What to do now?

I chose the Rainbow Room because it was a very public place and I would be safe. Fear of this charming intelligent stranger consumed me. Mother's stories flooded my brain. I called my friend Jack Serabian, an Armenian scholar, and got him out of bed with this plea: "Jack, you must help me, please come to the Rainbow Room right away. I'm with a Turk and I need a history lesson."

"But, Margaret, it's after midnight," Jack said.

"Please, Jack."

"I'll be there as fast as I can."

Jack arrived shortly. For the next two hours, these two scholars of history exchanged ideas. Each gave his version of the events with knowledge and understanding. Jack had parents who were deported from the very province that the diplomat's grandfather had reigned over. They even knew some of each other's friends and neighbors. I listened carefully to the wisdom and gracious interchange that transpired: no anger, no recriminations, no fear. What was wrong with me? Why couldn't I behave like this? Had Mother tainted my life with the bits and pieces of her stories? Ali invited me to visit Turkey. He said he could help me locate Mother's house in Amasia. He also said it would be unwise for me to travel alone in Turkey with an Armenian name on my passport.

"It would just not be safe, Margaret. Let me help you find your mother's house. You can trust me," he said.

"Trust no one." Mother's words, handed down to her from her brother Haroutoun, rang in my ears.

"Thank you," I said. "I'll be in touch."

Grasping my hand and not letting go, he replied, "I anxiously await your call."

In 1995, my husband, Bob, announced he had booked passage for us to Turkey.

"Turkey! I can't. I won't," I pleaded. "It's not safe for Armenians. Don't you remember the story I told you about Ali, the Turkish diplomat I met in New York?"

"No, I don't remember. Are we going or not? Wait a minute, I do remember. Why don't you call him?"

"Don't be silly, that must have been twenty years ago. I haven't any idea where he is today."

Again, Bob said, "Well, are we going or not? Besides your name is Ahnert now, there's nothing Armenian about that name!"

My dear sweet husband just didn't get it. With so much to explain, it was easier to say, "Okay, you win, I'll go to Turkey." He grinned with satisfaction. Bob liked to win.

At Kusadasi, Turkey, we hired a car and driver and an English-speaking tour guide. She was young, beautiful, and utterly charming; she spoke her memorized text fluidly. She brought the listener up through years of Turkish history. She mentioned the architecture of Ani and referred to some of the famous old churches as early examples of Ottoman architecture. From books I'd read, I knew that these churches were designed by Greek and Armenian architects.

When she got to 1915, our guide said, "In 1915, all the Greeks and Armenians living in Turkey simultaneously decided to go back to their own countries and left en masse."

The official Turkish tour guide told this story to every group every day. I quickly wrote down what she said, fearing I would not remember the exact wording.

She leaned over my shoulder and asked why I was writing down what she said. "Because I want to be sure I will remember it correctly," I replied.

She read my writing and proudly announced, "Yes, that's right, you have it right."

The killing of a culture was still going on.

Thinking of this now, I could see what purposes Mother's memories served me. And the world, too. Yes, it's good to be able to block things out. But maybe the terrible images persist for a reason: to tell the truth. Which is a terrible and terribly important thing.

SIXTEEN

JOURNEY TO AMERICA

ESTER — SUMMER 1920

The summer of 1920, our papers in order, we packed our personal belongings. We left behind all household goods, because we would be living with Heidi, the Zovickians' oldest daughter, in her flat on Riverside Drive in Manhattan.

We traveled by wagon from Amasia to Samsun. There we changed to another wagon for the journey to Constantinople. From Constantinople we sailed to Athens. In Athens we boarded the Greek liner, *Megalorelass*. Gretel and Bedros Effendi were in first class, and Eva, Sophia, Aram, and I were in third class.

As we climbed the gangway, a tall man in a white uniform

with gold braids on his shoulders announced loudly, "This way to steerage." He pointed to a steep stairwell off to the right.

"What's steerage?" I asked Aram.

Sensing my question, the man answered, "You'll find out soon enough, missy; it's the basement of the ship." He laughed heartily.

Gretel, clutching her ever-ready hanky, muttered, "Oh, I'm so sorry we couldn't all be together in first class."

There were hundreds of people on the dock. Some were sailing. Some were seeing friends and relatives off. Others just wanted to see the big ship up close. There was music, balloons and picnic baskets filled with food for the onlookers. There was shouting and waving as the ship slowly pushed away from the pier.

Aram, Eva, Sophia, and I climbed down the narrow, steep stairway, which was dark and slippery, to steerage. At the bottom we saw people lying in bunks that were stacked up one on top of the other. There wasn't enough room for a person to sit up in bed.

The smell of body odor hung over the room like a thick fog. Our space was up in the bow. I learned later that this was the worst place to be in a rough sea. Each of us was handed a woolen blanket. A young man in a blue uniform pointed to a specific spot.

"Over there, that's your place," he said.

I shook my blanket before wrapping it around me. A stream of roaches fell from the folds. Sophia and Eva screamed. Aram stepped on the roaches as they scurried in all directions. He jumped and stomped but there was no end to the little creatures. We had no pillows. The children and I rested one upon the other in a heap of body softness.

During the daylight hours, if the seas were calm, we were allowed on the outside decks, where the sun was warm and comforting. The soft ocean breezes swept away the ugly smells from our bodies. A young man from Czechoslovakia played happy polka music on his accordion day and night. Many screamed at him to shut him up but he paid no attention and played on.

One afternoon, a handsome blond-haired boy, who looked about my age, took my hand and tried to lead me towards other dancing couples. Neither of us spoke the other's language so we just motioned to each other. I knew I didn't know how to dance, so I shook my head no.

The next day he came over again. This time, he took my hand in his and led me to an open space. I didn't resist. He was tall. I kept my eyes to the ground. He bent down and pushed his nose against mine.

He had the bluest eyes. They looked like bits of water stuck in his face. I wanted to sink inside the blue ocean of his pupils. He pushed me this way and that way to the beat of the music. At first I felt clumsy. Then he moved me closer to him and our bodies touched. Now we moved together to the beat of the music. I laughed and danced and laughed and danced. It was the first time I'd ever danced this way. Aram said he was going to tell his father that I had danced with a stranger. I swore him to secrecy and he never told.

At sundown, we returned to the dark, roach-filled pit. The journey took fifteen days in very rough seas, and I was seasick most of the time. Every day Aram dragged me from the lower bow to the second-class deck to breathe some fresh air. Years before, on summer days at our aikee, I had dreamed of faraway places. Standing at the rail, I relived that dream. The colorful horizon spread out endlessly beyond the rails before me. There was no land in sight, only sea and sky and huge waves crashing over the railings. The dark water seemed to go on forever. Again, I felt hopelessly small and alone. Having come so close to death so many times, I tested my fate over and over on that ship. As the waves crashed and water flooded across the decks, I leaned over the rail as far as I could. With one hand on the rail and one in the air I barely hung on. Each time, I'd lean a little farther. Who was I testing? God? I was crazy.

One night, there was a big storm and the boat rocked from side to side. A heavy stream of water slapped across the decks as we descended the stairs. I turned my head and saw a crewman slip and slide across the deck. He just slid on and on. Just when I thought he would go overboard, some other crewmen grabbed him by his ankles and dragged him below.

During the trip people huddled in corners and talked about America. Most had relatives they planned to live with. "You know the streets are paved with gold," one said.

"You're crazy!" another said. "There are no streets of gold."

"Yes, yes," still another said. "I know this is true because a cousin of mine told me so."

I wondered which of them was right.

Three times a day, we were given a bowl of hot pasty soup with one piece of thick bread. There was no place to bathe and the toilet was a small closet-like space with a hole in the floor. I ate very little because I didn't want to use the toilet.

The morning of the fifteenth day, Aram shook me roughly. "Ester, Ester, we're here! It's America! Come quickly, I can see the Statue of Liberty."

I caught the girls in my arms and climbed the stairs to the upper deck. People were crammed against the rails. Everyone wanted to see Lady Liberty to confirm that they had finally made it to America. Everyone shouted in their native tongues.

"There she is!" Aram pointed. I was pushed into the middle of the crowd by those behind me trying to get a better look. Mothers lifted their small children. People cried. Some even knew the words written on the bottom of the statue.

"Give me your tired, your poor, your huddled masses yearning to breathe free." I tilted my head between someone's arm and shoulder. Yes, there she was towering above the boat in the morning mist. Then I was shoved away by another who was aching to see the grand lady. I didn't care. I had seen enough to confirm that I had indeed made it to America. I leaned back against the cold, black wall of the ship. I raised my face to the sky and whispered, *Asdvadz eem!* — My God.

The ship anchored in New York harbor. The first- and second-class passengers were the first to board the ferryboats headed to Ellis Island. Many passengers were nervous and worried that they would not pass the tough health inspectors. They knew that if they failed, they would be sent back to the country they came from. Bedros Effendi bribed someone to sneak us up to the first-class deck so that we could all leave the ship together. We were lucky. The rest of the third-class passengers got to Ellis Island by way of a separate clinic where, we were told, the doctors examined them more closely.

Aram said that one of the crewmembers told him that most of the people in third class would not make it to Ellis Island from that clinic.

"They won't? Where will they go?" I asked.

"They'll be shipped back to the country they came from if they're carrying a disease, and most of them down there are."

I hurried to get out of the hole full of sickness. I wondered if I was carrying a mysterious disease. Would I be found out? Would I be sent back? I bit my lip.

As we got off the ferry I couldn't believe all the noise. People were hurrying and yelling to one another. Men in blue uniforms with gold buttons shouted orders.

Then I heard, "Hey, you, over there, this way."

Did he mean me? Does he know that I am not Margaret Zovickian, the name on the passport? I lowered my head and moved ahead with the family. I breathed a sigh of relief when I realized it was not me he was talking to. We pressed together and moved forward slowly.

It was only a short distance from the ferry to the main building. The building was red brick, with stone trim and four tall towers. It looked like a castle in one of my storybooks. Once inside the main building, many left their suitcases in a room set aside for baggage on the first floor. We did not. We carried everything with us. We weren't taking any chances of losing our belongings. No one talked. We climbed up the steep staircase with many others like a big caterpillar inching its way along a tree branch.

I sucked in my breath as we passed a line of men in white coats standing by the rail, carefully looking at everyone as they passed. Anyone who looked like he had something wrong with him had his coat marked with chalk.

I learned later that they were the doctors who decided whether or not you stayed in America. The chalk mark L stood for lameness, H for heart disease, X for a possible mental illness. The people with chalk marks on their shoulders were taken out of line. The rest of us moved to a large room some-one called "The Registry Room."

Our family made it through the first inspection. The noisy room was filled with rows and rows of wooden benches. At the top of the high ceiling there were great big windows. I saw the clearest blue sky streaked with yellow stripes. Birds flew freely in and out of the yellow ribbon-like streaks. People were praying out loud in different languages. Some were on their knees; some were standing, hands clasped, heads tilted to the sky. Like the sound of a choir, murmured prayers of gratitude filled the hall.

We moved to a room where a clerk looked into my eyes with a magnifying glass. He asked me to put my hands out in front of me. He looked at both sides before he said, to no one in particular, "This one's okay."

I made it. But Bedros Effendi didn't.

I heard the doctor say, "This one stays. He has *bono. Bono,* the dreaded eye disease." *What will happen to us without Bedros Effendi?* I thought.

Then the doctor said, "The rest of you go through that door marked 'Push To New York.'"

None of us could read, but we knew how to follow. Holding Sophia's and Eva's hands tightly, Aram and I followed Frieda, who followed the crowd.

She turned to Bedros Effendi and cried, "What will I do? Where will you be?"

"Don't worry. I'll be with you soon," he said.

I remembered that's what my father said the last time I saw him.

We were directed to another ferry where there were more men in uniform and pushing people. As we came through the second terminal we found ourselves in the middle of a busy street filled with horses, wagons, and people.

"Oh, there's Heidi," Gretel shouted. "Here, over here, Heidi! Here we are."

I saw Heidi. Though I had heard Bedros Effendi and Gretel talk about her many times, I was not prepared for what I saw. She was standing by a long car Gretel called a limousine.

Heidi was wearing an ankle-length flowered silk dress. A gentle breeze folded the silk in layers around her long legs and thin body. A big straw hat with colored flowers spilling along the brim hid her face. Her hands were covered with delicate white lace gloves and her pale colored shoes were tightly laced up to her ankles. A yellow lace purse hung from her thin wrist.

"Over here, Mother, come this way," she waved. Gretel crossed the street and hugged her daughter. The girls, Sophia and Eva, jumped to hug Heidi too, but she gave them a quick hug and said, "You're so sweaty and dirty. Hurry! Let's get away from these crowds and get you all cleaned up."

Aram nudged me to enter the car. Before I got in, I bent down and pressed my lips to the hard dirt surface. It smelled of manure and cigarettes. Heidi was embarrassed and quickly pushed me into the car.

"You must be Ester," she said. "Now stop that — you look like a greenhorn."

"What's a greenhorn?"

"You are," she answered. "Get in the car."

The immigration people kept Bedros Effendi for two days in the clinic to see if his eyes would heal with the right medicine. He was lucky the liquid they gave him worked. They let him go.

Heidi's apartment on Riverside Drive had a doorman and ten rooms filled with antique furniture. Heidi thought that Bedros was arriving with lots of gold and money and the fine rugs and furniture from the house in Amasia. What she did not know was that he spent most of his savings for the passage and additional bribes needed to obtain the papers for us to leave without delay. There was lots of yelling and screaming about the rent and the lack of money. I stayed out of the way with the girls in a back bedroom.

After several moves we settled in an apartment at 180th Street and Third Avenue. I took care of the children, cooked, and did embroidery at home. Several months later Bedros Effendi got me a job at Edwardian's Embroidery Factory. Every day after straightening the apartment and fixing breakfast I took the elevated train to the factory.

At lunchtime, Mairam, a short chubby girl from Sivas, and I were sent by Mr. Edwardian to buy fruit at Albert Ajemian's produce store just a few doors away. Albert handed me a shiny red apple. When I reached for it he held it tight. He would not let it go. Then he bent over and stared at my face. Did he know me? Would he turn me in to the police because he knew I was not Margaret Zovickian? No, he was just looking at a pretty young girl. Things were really different here in America.

"What's your name?" he asked.

I stopped, thought for a moment about saying Margaret, then quickly decided I didn't want to lie to my new friend.

"Ester," I said. "My name is Ester."

Albert tilted his head and slowly mouthed the word, "Ester."

I liked the sound of his voice. He had a nice smile.

"Where do you girls come from?" he asked.

We giggled, but did not answer.

"Do you have tongues?" he shouted.

We held our hands over our mouths to hold back our laughter. Every day, Mairam and I stopped at Albert's store during our short breaks. I began to look forward to these daily visits.

The hours at Edwardian's were long and though Mr. Edwardian was nice enough, he was always telling the girls to sew faster and produce more. We were paid by the piece, so the more we embroidered the more money we made and the more money Mr. Edwardian made. He would march up and down the row of sewing machines waving his arms like a bandleader. He wore a funny brown wool hat, summer and winter. He wiped his brow with a dirty hanky. Leftovers of whatever he had for lunch were usually still sticking to the limp hairs of his moustache.

"Come on, girls, stop talking and get to work. I'm not running a house of charity here. I need to earn a living and so do you," he'd say, wiping his nose with the back of his hand.

We'd race our machines at full steam. When the loud whizzing sound reached a high pitch, Edwardian smiled. But as soon as he left the room, we'd slow down to gossip.

Mairam and I held hands and walked to Albert's store everyday. Funny, I never saw Mairam in Sivas, yet here we were in America working in the same factory. She was living with a Turk in Sivas, as I was, but our paths had never crossed.

After we'd made our fruit purchases Albert followed us a while, chanting, *bazeh, bazeh yegek*. This phrase was funny because it was a mixture of Turkish and Armenian. *Bazeh, bazeh* in Turkish means "from time to time" and yegek in Armenian means "come." He was saying, "Come and see me from time to time."

Years later, we'd laugh about those days.

Albert would say, "You know, I said *bazeh, bazeh yegek,* come and visit once in a while, but you came and fell on me."

Then he'd thoughtfully say, "I'm glad you came and stayed. Yes, I'm glad you did."

In the evening, Aram and I went to classes to learn English. One night, as we left school, Albert was waiting outside. I wanted to see him. Again, I swore Aram to secrecy. Every night Albert and I talked for a while at a nearby coffee shop.

Albert told me that he was born in 1895, in the town of Dirvig. He said his father had been an interpreter for the Turkish government in Constantinople and spoke Turkish, Italian, Greek, and English, in addition to his native tongue, Armenian. Albert also had one sister, but after he left the country he lost contact with her. He told me he was in the Turkish army before he escaped to Constantinople from Dirvig to join his father.

Sitting in the coffee shop one night, Albert said, "You know, when I was living in Constantinople in 1919, many of my Greek friends there were told they would soon be deported. One day, as my father and I walked down the street, a lady accused me of being Greek, because I spoke the language so well. My father was so afraid that I might be immediately shipped out to a death camp, he quickly put together new paperwork so I could leave right away. He said he would follow shortly.

"I arrived in America a few months later. I never saw my father, mother, or sister again. I had some money saved. With it, I opened the small produce store where you met me."

A few months later, as we sat in the coffee shop, Albert took my hand in his and said, "Ester, let's get married."

I didn't hesitate. I secretly had been waiting for the question and my answer was ready. I tilted my head to one side, carefully watching his face and said, "Yes, Albert, I will marry you." He smiled.

Albert bought me an ivory lace dress and veil. We were married on April 24, 1921, at the Armenian Church on 28th Street in New York. Poor Albert, he had to overcome the council of the church who refused to marry us. They said marriages could not be performed during Lent. They also had a second reason. April 24th was the anniversary of the genocide. Only six years had passed since that "drive of death."

I begged Albert not to give in to the council, because, in my heart, I believed that if we changed the date, we would never marry. Albert paid the clerk extra money and we were married as planned.

My Papa had loved me. Grandmom, Pepron, and Vartouhi had loved me. With Albert, I was loved once again.

I cannot explain why I didn't die like many of the others. We are born, we suffer, we laugh and we die. *'Asdvadz keedeh,'* only God knows.

The one thing I know for certain is that, because I survived, I wanted to bring new life into the world. I wanted to pass on the strong, rich blood that flowed in my veins. I wanted my family blood to carry on for generations. If God granted me daughters, I would name one Margaret, in honor of the dead girl whose passport I had used to escape.

EPILOGUE

MARGARET – FEBRUARY 6, 1999

When Bob and I arrived on Bimini in time to tie up and have dinner, there were just a few fishing boats in the marina. Not many boats venture through the rough February seas to fish. But rough waters never deterred us; we'd been fishing these waters for over 20 years.

Always pleasant, the locals greeted us at the dock as though we were visiting family.

"Hey, mon, nice to see you back again. You stayin' long?"

Our answer was always the same. "As long as we catch fish we'll stay." As though we could determine fish catching.

The next morning, I got on my bike and hurried out to The Pines. I felt especially close to my mother that day, close and uneasy. I was still shaken by a nightmare I had had the night before. In my sleep, I had cried, "My mother is dead, my mother is dead." Bob held me close, but when I did not wake, he shook me hard. "Margaret, wake up, you're having a bad dream. Your mother is not dead."

"But it's so real, it must be true."

"Now listen, it's a nightmare," Bob said. "It's 2 A.M. No one has come to the boat with any messages. Go back to sleep, it was just a bad dream, your mother is fine."

I slept fitfully the rest of the night. At 8 A.M., I headed for the marina office. I direct dialed mother's room at the home. No answer. She must be having breakfast in the dining room, I thought. I'll call again after my walk on the beach.

It's a twenty-minute bike ride to the northern tip of the island, a half-mile past The Pines. I parked my bike and headed for the beach only yards away. I was alone.

I walked the empty beach. Beneath my feet was pristine white sand kissed by the aqua blue sea, flecked with white foam. I could almost hear Mother's voice.

"Don't lean against a cold wall. Germs will enter your body and you will get sick."

It was a cool February day in the Bahamas, but the likelihood of my finding a cold wall to lean on was little to none.

Walking on the cool sand, I wondered about the dream I'd had, it had seemed so real. *I'll fly to New York in a couple of days and Mother will smile, as she always does, when she sees me arriving with a new flower arrangement.* I took a quick swim in the chilly water and headed back for some hot coffee.

The three-mile bike ride back to the marina went quickly. There was no traffic on the narrow road. When I stopped at the office again to call Mother, Denise at the front desk handed me a telephone message.

"Call this number," she said. I recognized the number of the Armenian Home. I quickly dialed.

"This is Margaret Ahnert, I'm calling about my mother, Ester." There was a long pause before I was connected to the nurse's station.

"Oh, Mrs. Ahnert, your mother died this morning, didn't someone call you?"

"What, what did you say? When did this happen, why?"

"Your mother had an irregular heartbeat and the doctor thought she should be looked at. She was admitted to the hospital for observation. I'm told she slept well, had a large breakfast, closed her eyes, and died. I am so sorry. I thought you knew."

"No, no," I dropped the phone. Denise came around the desk, pulled me to her chest and held me tight. I remembered when Papa died and I sobbed into the breasts of a large woman. I was thirteen again. Swivel, swivel, the clock turns.

I thought of Mother's Amasia family. Haroutoun, Pepron, Hajji Hagop, her grandmother, Vartouhi, Arsen, all gone. I imagine my mother united with her family, and my father is there, too. They are all together now, amongst the clouds, perhaps somewhere near Mt. Ararat.

I think I hear her voice, *Bou da getchere*. This, too, shall pass. In a few weeks, Mother would have been ninety-nine.

I think of my children, my grandchildren, what do they know of Ester? They know about her life and they know she loved them. They know about the blood we share, our DNA. What more is there to know?

foreign languages as they pushed their way toward the rail for a better view.

I thought of Mother on the *Megalorelass,* the ship that brought her to America, and the multitude of languages spoken that day. I said to Lynn, "This will be the first time Sara sees the statue, just as Mother did when she arrived in 1920."

Sara's bright eyes scanned the horizon. She wanted to be the first of us to see the vision. As the ship rolled away from the dock, I reached into my purse and unraveled four pages of my manuscript. I handed them to Sara.

"This is the chapter that tells how Great Grandmom felt the first time she saw Lady Liberty."

Sara silently read the pages, then looked up at me and said, "I never knew how Great Grandmom felt the day she arrived in America, did she tell you all this, Grammy?"

I smiled, "Yes, Sara, your Great Grandmom was an amazing woman. She remembered many details about her life."

"No stops here," a voice announced over the loudspeaker. "Take your pictures now."

I overheard someone say that since September 11, 2001, visitors are prohibited from walking around the grounds surrounding the statue or climbing the long, winding staircase inside. I squeezed the handrail and swallowed hard. I remembered the yearly school trips I had taken to the island with my New York classmates. Laughing and pushing each other, we'd climb the narrow stairs to the top of the crown and even higher into Lady Liberty's arm. From this lofty space I could see New Jersey, New York City, and Long Island. Sara and her generation have been robbed of this experience. It's a strange time we live in. Mother lived in fear of her life in Turkey until she reached the safety of American soil. Now we live in fear of terrorists from distant shores.

As we disembarked on Ellis Island, I walked apart from Sara and Lynn, needing to feel my mother's spirit, needing to feel what she had felt. I walked slowly, as I envisioned Mother had, moving with the crowd, my head down. Externally, the building was the same as Mother had described it to me: red brick, four towers reaching for the sky. The great, open windows were now sealed and the building was air-conditioned. The birds that flew in and out of the chamber that day in 1920 could no longer enter the hall to fly over our heads as they did when Ester and her family had arrived. The long narrow staircase was gone. I asked a guard, "Which way to the wall of names?"

"Out the back door and to the left," he said. Sara and Lynn joined me as we headed toward the rear of the building.

Out in the sunshine, blue skies and crystal-clear blue water dramatically offset the long, serpentine wall. There were only a few people milling about. "They're not here," I whispered. I scanned all the incised rows in a desperate effort to find Ester's and Albert's names. "But I sent in a check for two names to be listed," I said to no one in particular.

"Don't be upset, Grammy, we'll find them. They must be here," Sara said, trying to sound comforting.

Fifteen minutes passed. We checked the wall from beginning to end, again and again, nothing. Lynn suggested the computer terminal she saw near the entrance.

"I hate computers, they run the world." By the time I got to the computer attendant, I was sobbing. "My mother and father are not listed. I paid," I sputtered. "I don't understand."

"Now, now, calm down," said the lady at the desk with ruby-red lips and dark rolled-up hair. "Let's look in the computer."

I took a deep breath. Everything is computerized these days, even my mother. "Yes, here they are," the woman said.

"Where, where? I could not find their names."

"There is a second wall around the building, your mother and father are in that section. Try there. I'm sure you'll find your parents."

I ran in the direction she was pointing, Sara and Lynn on my heels. On the first panel a short way down in the A's I saw Albert Ajemian. Just under Papa's name was Ester Ahronian Ajemian. I rubbed my fingers gently over the letters. My chest hurt. I was shaking. The Turkish government tried to extinguish my mother from the face of the earth, but she prevailed, her name etched into this wall next to her beloved Albert forever. Sara hugged me; I felt her tears on my skin. Lynn circled her arms around us both. We stood this way for a long while. I could feel Ester. "It's okay, Mother, you are safe, you are in America and we are here with you."

Sometimes, I think I see my mother taking her afternoon walk on the street where I live. Often, I reach for the phone to dial her at the Armenian Home, a daily habit; some rituals are hard to break.

I think of Oscar Wilde, who once said, "The truth is rarely pure and never simple."

I believe Ester rests having told her truth.

IN LOVING MEMORY

ESTER MINERAJIAN AHRONIAN AJEMIAN

MARCH 12, 1900–FEBRUARY 7, 1999

GLOSSARY

N.B.: Some of the Turkish and Armenian words are spelled phonetically, the way Ester related them to Margaret.

abour: soup
aikee: summer home built in an orchard
ambar: container
amsagan: menstruation
anoonovet dzeranas: grow old with your name
Asdvadz: God
Asvadzeem: my God
atchigess: my daughter
azadey: save
baksheesh: graft
bazeh: once in a while
basterma: cured beef
bono: eye disease
boobegh: cookie
booduks: bins

bou da getchere: this, too, shall pass
burug: covering worn by Muslim women
char: bad
chay-bashi: superior farmland
choreg: bread
davoul: drum
der-der: priest
dosheg: feather quilt
dohn: name day
erigah: husband
geshoud: dried dung
giavour: infidel
guhneega: wife
haidey: hurry
henayeum: red dye on bride
Imam: Muslim priest
Jami: Muslim church
janum: little one
karouma: fried lamb
kese: scrub brush like a loofa
keshgeg: lamb with barley
kouyrig: sister
Kurd der vourar: It is a Kurd that strikes
lahmajun: meat pizza
maghazan: basement
mayrig: mother
mortseer: to forget
oghee: whiskey
paree: good
sadir: sofa
scambeel: card game
seeroum: sweet one

senavat: wine pressing tub
Seni öldüreyim mi?: Shall I kill you?
Sepastatsi: person from Sivas
soorp: holy
soujouk: cured beef
tahn: yogurt drink
toneer: cooking pit
toot: mulberry
tourshee: pickles
tzakgiss: my child
vailey: enjoy
varbed: teacher
Vartevar: holiday in April
vishneh: mulberry jam
yallah: hurry
yayligee: wagon driver
yegek: come
yemeni: a kind of peasant slipper
yorgan: blanket
zaptiyehs: soldiers
zourna: flute

ACKNOWLEDGMENTS

I wish to thank the following for their caring contributions to this book: Dr. James Wolff and Janet Wolff, whose constant friendship buoyed me through the long years of writing. Suzanne Young and Sarah Lucie, my editors, whose help was immeasurable; Lauren Slater, my Goucher professor who provided greater insight; Marjorie Dobkin Hovesepian, who saw the earliest draft and encouraged me not to quit. Emilie Jacobson and Dave Barbour at Curtis Brown, who stayed with me; Aram Arkum at the Zorhab Information Center of the Diocese of the Armenian Church, whose knowledge of the Turkish language and history helped me immensely. My publisher, Margot Atwell, for her encouragement and belief in my mission to tell the world about the Armenian Genocide, which led to many printings and this paperback. My children, Lynn Price and Steven Sarajian, who supported my determination and worried about my safety. My sometimes bodyguard and very special love, Edward Odabashian, for always being there for me. My grandchildren, Raymond and Sara, who were blessed by Ester's love, and my dear late husband, Bob, who supported me tirelessly throughout the writing process and loved Ester as much as he loved me. Thanks also to the late Governor Hugh L. Cary and Robert Morganthau, whose thoughts about the Armenian Genocide helped bring my mother's story to the page. Many thanks to my dear friends Berge and Vera Setrakian, Dr. José Sarukhan, Alain Terzian, Garnik Nanagoulian, Levon Lachikyan Ragip Zarakolu, Hayk Demoyan, Dr. Christine Wheeler, and last but never least, Leigh Giroux, my outstanding literary attorney.

ABOUT THE TYPE

This book is set in Sabon. Designed in the 1960s by Jan Tschichold, Sabon was commissioned by a consortium of the German printing industry, who wanted a new text typeface that would suitable for all printing purposes. The new typeface was to look for its roots and inspiration to the sixteenth-century types of the French typecutter Claude Garamond, but to be a practical modern-day text face. Tschichold designed very few typefaces, and Sabon was his masterwork; it has become a modern classic.

ABOUT THE AUTHOR

MARGARET AJEMIAN AHNERT was born in New York City. Growing up, she listened to her mother's stories about her own childhood during the Armenian Genocide in Turkey. She has a Master of Fine Arts and Literature from Goucher College and a BA from Goddard College, and is a graduate of the Barnes Foundation of Fine Arts, Merion, Pennsylvania. She has pursued a variety of careers: producing TV documentaries, lecturing as a docent at the Metropolitan Museum of Art and the Philadelphia Museum of Art, managing the Fernwood Resort and Hotel as co-owner, and teaching art appreciation through the Art Goes to School program in elementary schools. Ahnert holds a 100-ton master captain's license and is an avid hunter and fisherwoman.

Margaret Ajemian Ahnert has also founded a number of foundations, including The Robert Ahnert Memorial Foundation, which funds tuition for students at the Holy Name Catholic School in Bimini, Bahamas, and The Margaret Ajemian Ahnert Foundation in memory of her mother, Ester Ajemian, which funds scholarships for journalism students in Yerevan, Armenia.

Margaret was awarded the Ellis Island Medal of Honor on May 7, 2011 and the Honorable "Musa Dagh Battle" Medal in 2008. She is a member of the National League of American Pen Women. The Knock at the Door is the New York Book Festival's Best Historical Memoir of 2008, and USA Book News Best Book of 2007.